AFRICAN CHRISTIANITY

Adrian Hastings

A Crossroad Book
The Seabury Press • New York

The Seabury Press
815 Second Avenue
New York, N.Y. 10017

First published in the U.K. by Geoffrey Chapman,
a division of Cassell & Collier Macmillan Publishers Ltd.

Printed in the United States of America

Library of Congress Cataloging in Publication Data

Hastings, Adrian.
    African Christianity.
    "A Crossroad book."
    Bibliography: p.
    Includes index.
    1. Christianity—Africa. I. Title.
BR1360.H3   209'.6   77-1890
ISBN 0-8164-0336-8

The author wishes to acknowledge passages
quoted from the following sources: Bengt
Sundkler, *Bantu Prophets in South Africa,*
Oxford University Press; Jacques Louis Hymans,
*Léopold Sédar Senghor: An Intellectual Bio-
graphy,* Edinburgh University Press; Walter
H. Sangree, *Age, Prayer and Politics in Tiriki,
Kenya,* Oxford University Press; Aylward Shorter,
African Culture and the Christian Church,
Geoffrey Chapman; and Ann Spence for verses from
an unpublished paper.

Contents

Preface   v

1 A century of growth   1
2 Ministries, missionaries and moratorium   17
3 Cultural revolution   37
4 Patterns of healing   60
5 Power, politics and poverty   77

References and further reading   97

Index   103

For
BENGT SUNDKLER
Ecumenical Bishop
Mzee

Preface

The Christian Churches in Africa are both a vital element in the life of that continent and the most quickly growing sector within world Christianity. It is hoped that a wide ranging discussion of their main concerns, problems and achievements by someone who has shared their life for many years but is yet, finally, an outside interpreter may meet a need both inside and outside Africa.

This book could not have been written without two years of seminars at the School of Oriental and African Studies, London, and a major conference at Jos, Nigeria, in September 1975 on Christianity in Independent Africa. Participants in these discussions will, I am sure, recognise a hundred times how the thinking of this book has grown out of the general flow of papers and conversation, and I must express the deepest debt of gratitude to all those who have made both the SOAS seminars and Jos Conference possible and so stimulating. My own participation as a Research Officer of the School has depended on a grant from the Leverhulme Foundation; both to the Foundation and to the School of Oriental and African Studies for sponsoring the entire programme I am most grateful.

The present book is only, we trust, a small part of the fruits of the programme; it is intended that a selection of the papers from both seminars and the Conference at Jos will also be published, as well as a more extended treatment of the history of Christianity in Africa over the last twenty-five years. But it is hoped that the present book will respond particularly to the wishes of some of the bodies who have supported the programme, both morally and financially, by providing a wider public with something of a readable synthesis in a field almost too bewildering with its richness and complexity.

To close, I must say a very special word of appreciation to Professor Richard Gray, who directed the whole programme, persuaded me to take part in it originally, later proposed that I write this book, and finally read it through chapter by chapter. It is, of course, finally my responsibility alone, but of this book it can be said with certainty that without Richard's friendship and constant encouragement it would never have existed.

6 February 1976   Adrian Hastings

CHAPTER 1

A century of growth

The fifth assembly of the World Council of Churches meeting in Africa, in Nairobi during November 1975, proclaimed by its very location, and still more by a large proportion of its participants and the theme of many of its discussions, one simple and significant fact: the Christian churches are today thriving in Africa as almost nowhere else. The era of 'missions', in which Christianity in Africa was seen as a plant which had hardly taken root, which needed constant care from outside, which it was a duty to instruct but to which one would certainly not expect to listen—that era is over.

Today there are at least ninety million Christians on the continent of Africa and the number is steadily growing. The Copts in Egypt, the Orthodox Church of Ethiopia continue as they have done for over fifteen hundred years. The Roman Catholic Church has more than three hundred dioceses across the length and breadth of Africa. Anglicans, Lutherans, Methodists, Presbyterians, Baptists, Pentecostals, all have strong churches in one or another part of the continent; and then there are the new denominations—Kimbanguists and Aladura, Eden Revival and Maria Legio, Zionists and Ethiopians, prophetic churches, praying churches, healing churches, all founded by Africans during the last hundred years and now with millions of adherents of their own. The life and death of the Zairean prophet Simon Kimbangu; the lonely witness at Lambarene hospital in Gabon of that ascetic but obstinate theologian, musician and doctor, Albert Schweitzer, until his death in 1965 at the age of ninety; the turbulent career of Alice Lenshina in Zambia; the communist-capitalist success story of the 'Happy City', the Holy Apostles Community at Aiyetoro in a Nigerian coastal lagoon; the World Council grants to African Liberation Movements and the emergence of Black Theology; philosopher kings such as Léopold Senghor and Julius Nyerere; the heroically consistent and restrained witness against *apartheid* of the Dutch Reformed

Predikant, Beyers Naudé—what riches and complexity are to be found here! The modern African church has had its prophets and visionaries, its kings and its priests, its strategists, its martyrs, its vociferous spokesmen, its innumerable humble worshippers.

It is safe to say that in no other continent during the last fifty years has Christianity shown so much growth and diversity, such a cheerful but perplexing flood of people confidently doing their own thing, often in seemingly strange and contradictory ways. And yet, just one hundred years ago, African Christianity only barely existed. In 1875, it is true, the state church of Ethiopia and the Coptic Church of Egypt were already as old and venerable as any church throughout the world, but they were in no way in contact with the rest of the continent. Elsewhere there were a few Christian communities scattered along the coasts of Africa, particularly in the south and west, but most inland parts had never known the gospel preached in any form.

On the West Coast from Senegal to the Niger a network of sturdy little churches, Anglican, Methodist, Presbyterian and Catholic, now existed. They were the fruit of black Christians returning from the Americas, and of the brief efforts of white missionaries from Europe destined in nearly every case for an early grave. The men who really carried the Christian faith along the West Coast in the mid-nineteenth century were nearly all Africans, many of them men and women rescued from slave ships on the Atlantic and landed by the British navy at Freetown. One of the most remarkable of the pioneer missionaries was never a slave, though his father had been. Thomas Birch Freeman had a Negro father and an English mother. Born in England, his fifty years of service on the Gold Coast—begun at a time when most of his fellow missionaries lived hardly fifty weeks—did much to establish Methodism as the most deeply rooted church of southern Ghana.

The best known Christian pioneer of that age was undoubtedly Samuel Ajayi Crowther. A Yoruba, he was rescued as a boy of fifteen from a slave ship in 1822, was educated by CMS missionaries in Freetown and then himself became a teacher at their college of Fourah Bay before returning to his own country of Nigeria as a missionary. In 1864 he was consecrated bishop in Canterbury Cathedral—the first African bishop of the Anglican communion. His diocese was vast, the whole of West Africa outside the small existing British colonies being initially entrusted to him though in fact he concentrated on the lower Niger; but as the white missionaries were not willing to serve under him they continued to be responsible to the English Bishop of Sierra Leone. Eleven years later, in May 1875, one elderly missionary, David Hinderer, wrote: 'Has not the time come when the native bishop's jurisdiction should be further extended than the Niger, especially to his own native soil?' However, the tide was to flow the other way. Despite Crowther's patient and conscientious work across the years, white missionaries both on the spot and in England increasingly distrusted him, believing that his appointment had been essentially a mistake: the reins of power should be kept firmly in efficient white hands for an indefinite period. At the time most missionaries tended to despise both African culture and African capacity. They believed that the Christian religion must go with a European culture and European leadership. Already African Christians were becoming conscious of this contempt, resented it and frequently saw the future of African Christianity in a very different way.

By 1875 there was then an African Christian society in being along the West Coast, from the Catholic Church in Senegal at one end to Bishop Crowther's diocese on the lower Niger at the other. In southern Africa too, besides the white settler churches— Dutch Reformed, Anglican, Methodist—in the western Cape, Grahamstown and on the high veld, missionaries had been active for many years among some Africans not only on the coast but far inland. Robert Moffat, of the London Missionary Society and David Livingstone's father-in-law, was the great pioneer north of the Orange River. From his headquarters at Kuruman he travelled widely over what is now Botswana and Rhodesia. French Evangelicals and Roman Catholics vied with one another among the Basuto in their mountains, while nearer the coast churches were multiplying particularly among the Xhosa people. By 1875 the great Khama, baptised twelve years before, was chief of the Bamangwato. The pride of the London Missionary Society, he was to establish the dominance of Congregationalism and abstinence from alcohol among his people.

Four years before, in September 1871, Tiyo Soga, the Presbyterian, first minister of the Xhosa people, had died from fever contracted during his pastoral journeying. Educated for some years in Scotland, he had become a superb writer of hymns, the translator of *Pilgrim's Progress* as of parts of the Bible, and a singularly ecumenical figure. He was known as an indefatigable preacher and pastor, a lover of all men whatever their denomina-

3

tion, a renowned master of language and the pride of his people. As he lay dying he continued with his translation of the *Acts of the Apostles*, finally laying down the work at the end of chapter 23 with a simple scribbled note of explanation 'I have lost strength'. As witness to the African Christianity of a century ago he stands for the south as Crowther stands for the west.

Further north there was almost nothing. The old Portuguese missions on both the West Coast and the east had almost disappeared by this time, leaving behind a few buildings, many of them more or less in ruins, and a pitiful handful of clergy to minister to the small white or half-white colonial population. Livingstone died in the northern part of what is now Zambia in 1873 and as yet next to nothing had been done to spread the gospel to central Africa beyond a few coastal mission stations—the CMS at Mombasa, the Holy Ghost Fathers at Bagamoyo. The expedition of the Universities Mission to Central Africa led by Bishop Mackenzie to the Lower Shiré in the early 1860s had been forced quickly to withdraw after Mackenzie's death. Yet 1875 was to be the most significant date for the start of a new penetration. It was the year in which a Scottish Presbyterian party set out to establish the mission of Livingstonia on the shores of Lake Malawi; it included Robert Laws who was to be the presiding genius of Livingstonia, perhaps the most decisively influential institution in the whole of central Africa, and he would still be at work there in the 1930s.

In 1875 too the Universities Mission to Central Africa decided that the time was ripe for a new venture to the interior and struck inland from Zanzibar to Magila in the hill country of northern Tanzania. Two years later the first CMS missionaries reached the court of King Mutesa of Buganda to be followed within a few months by the White Fathers of Cardinal Lavigerie.

That is how Christianity stood in Africa one hundred years ago: resolute beginnings but little more. If we now turn over fifty years and look at the scene again in 1925, what do we find? In the meantime the European powers—Great Britain, France, Belgium, Portugal and (until the first world war) Germany—have divided almost the entire continent between them. In 1875 Africa was a continent of hundreds of independent kingdoms, tribes, small republics, coastal colonies; an intricate political mosaic, which sometimes involved a political chaos. By 1925 the heavy hand of colonialism has sorted out all that, establishing at the same time a network of railways and roads which made the task of the missionary much less difficult. And the churches had spread almost as much as the empires. There were now some 7,000 Roman Catholic and 5,500 Protestant missionaries in Africa south of the Sahara, while the number of Christians was some five million as against perhaps half a million fifty years before. If the whole population was something in the order of 150 million in 1925, then about 3% was now Christian, and the number was growing fast. There were large areas, particularly those regarded as Moslem such as northern Nigeria, where missionaries were hardly permitted to enter but the accessible field before them was now vast indeed.

Most of the schools and hospitals which existed in black Africa in 1925 were run by missionaries, often with little support or encouragement from government, though the latter was just beginning to take a far greater interest in such things under the prodding of the Phelps–Stokes Commissions. Many missionaries were fine linguists, producing dictionaries and grammars for the main local languages as well as translating the Bible or other religious works. In one way and another missionaries and their collaborators were the great innovators in rural Africa in the 1920s. They had now the numbers, the expertise, the power to make a large scale impact not just upon the inhabitants of a few well-run mission villages and settlements but upon rural society as a whole. Of course the overall impact greatly varied, depending as it did upon the mysterious collective decision of a particular people to be interested or not. Many of the peoples of Africa still showed extremely little interest in these innovations which were bound to be so disruptive of their traditions, culture and social order; but others turned to them with alacrity. It was clear enough to them that the new 'western' order with its trains and taxes, its district commissioners and guns, its books and its curious medicines had come to stay; if so, it was vitally important to make sense of it all, to use the white man's things to advance oneself and stand up to the white man too.

In many places during the 19th century it tended to be the misfits in the old society or those who had come loose from it anyhow, such as the enslaved, who sought a home in the Christian churches. But the more the new order, political and economic, manifestly took over the very centre of society forcing the old establishment willy-nilly to conform to its ways, the stronger grew the social appeal of the ideology which went with this order— Christianity. It could provide a co-ordinating frame of reference for

5

the new world, and it could also provide a great many useful practical helps. If it's too late for me, at least let me send my son to school—and school meant baptism too. Becoming a Christian could bring considerable material advantages; essentially it brought one within the 'modern', 'progressive' sector of society—the sector with paid jobs such as teacher, clerk or lawyer. It went with wearing the white man's clothes and talking to him rather more as an equal. The pursuit whether of wealth, of wider knowledge or political power followed clearly enough the way of the Christian churches. Such factors of course can operate powerfully without always or, perhaps, generally being consciously recognised motives. People are caught up in a movement, impressed by a particular personality, or in need of a supporting community within a wider situation of social change. Many people who became Christian got little enough out of it in any worldly way, and they probably sought little too—some new assurance of protection, some glimmer of a wider horizon, some sharing in a new and apparently self-confident fellowship. The spiritual power and manifest generosity of missionaries and local pastors as men of God, wise advisers, defenders in distress together with the friendliness and sense of belonging engendered in the communities they founded were probably more decisive factors for the growth of the church than the establishment of schools and hospitals.

Certainly by 1925 the mission churches were riding high. The early pioneering period was over. With the firm establishment of colonial rule even in the most remote areas, with a growing practical collaboration between missions and governments (even in French Africa where the government had previously been decidedly anti-clerical and anti-missionary), with a manifestly increasing receptiveness to their influence on the part of Africans, the missionary societies were throwing everything into the field and felt still short of men. Yet, while much was done to recruit local assistants, catechists and junior native pastors, who were coming to bear the brunt of most pastoral and evangelistic work, there was very little thought at this time of handing over any major authority to local people. In the 19th century the rigours of the climate, the massive mortality rate among white missionaries, their still tiny number in all, the relative simplicity of the work envisaged, all this had encouraged some missionary leaders to think in terms of a fairly rapid handover to African churchmen: a handover which would be fully in accord with the best scriptural and early church precedent.

6

As the years passed, the need and the advisability of this appeared to diminish. Health problems were largely overcome and as missionaries lived longer and grew more numerous, they felt increasingly reluctant to transfer the control of their work to native hands. The very development of increasingly complex institutions appeared to justify this attitude: who could run all these things in the forseeable future except white men? Although in a few churches a local pastoral clergy with increasing experience was being steadily built up, there was by 1925 in most missionary circles an undoubted hardening in regard to any vigorous policy of Africanisation. When Bishop Crowther died in 1891 he was not replaced by another black diocesan bishop. In 1925 there were no African diocesan bishops in any mission church and remarkably few clergy except in rather inferior positions. This was more true of the Roman Catholic Church than of any other, but that was in part the consequence of its universal insistence upon a long seminary training and rather high educational standards for all priests. In places, however, the formation of a local leadership was going vigorously forward. Thus the Catholic Church in Buganda had ordained its first African priest, Victor Mukasa, in 1913 (he is still alive, active and an inspiration to many in 1976), and after him there was a steady stream of new Baganda priests. In this case much of the credit must be given to the very far-sighted and determined bishop of the area, the Alsatian Mgr Streicher. Out of his policy would emerge the first Catholic diocese to have an African bishop on the continent, Masaka in 1939. But it was very much an exception.

There were, of course, many outstanding African Christians within the mission churches in the 1920s. Let us recall a few of them. Apolo Kivebulaya was a very simple Anglican saint. A Muganda, baptised in 1895 and ordained a priest eight years later, he lived until death in 1933 an intensely ascetic, industrious and celibate life as a missionary at Mboga among the pygmies in the far west of Uganda. In 1925 David Kaunda, a Tonga Presbyterian educated at Livingstonia, had already been for many years headmaster of the school of Lubwa, in what is today northern Zambia, a pioneer missionary among the Bemba. A man of great zeal and wide influence, he was soon to return to Livingstonia for further training and ordination as the first African Presbyterian minister in the country. In 1925 his son Kenneth was just one year old.

Four years before J. Tengo Jabavu had died at Fort Hare in

7

South Africa. One of the great figures who owed their education to the Presbyterian centre of Lovedale in the Ciskei (the southern equivalent to Livingstonia) he was distinguished as journalist, politician, educationalist and churchman—a leader of his people right across the board, and a man still desperately anxious to work with white men rather than against them. He had struggled hard for the establishment of the University College of Fort Hare, became a member of its executive and died there. For many Africans it was quite simply *I—Koleji ka Jabavu*. His son was later to become its first African professor. As Tengo Jabavu lay dying and breathing grew more difficult, he witnessed with his last words to an African Christian spiritual tradition already flourishing as he slowly sang to himself Tiyo Soga's great hymn.

> Lizalis' idinga Lako
> Tixo, Nkosi yenyaniso,
> Zonk' intlanga zalo mhlaba
> Mazizuze usindiso.
>
> Fulfil Thy promises,
> O God, Lord of truth,
> Let every tribe of this land
> Obtain salvation.

The most prominent African figure of 1925 was without doubt the Ghanaian James Emman Kwegyir Aggrey. Born in 1875 he was now at the height of his powers. Twenty years of study in America had been followed by his travels right across Africa on the two Phelps–Stokes Commissions. A magnetic orator, a man of endless energy, humour and balance, he was the black world's ideal ambassador to the white, the white world's ideal ambassador to the black. D. D. T. Jabavu wrote after Aggrey's very brief South African visit in 1921: 'Without doubt he has done more than any other visitor I know of, in the brief space of time, to persuade people in our circumstances of the necessities of racial co-operation between white and black.' Offered a Professorship at Fort Hare and the post of President of Livingstone College in North Carolina where he had studied, he refused both to work as Assistant Vice-Principal of the new college of Achimota in his own Gold Coast. That was where he was in 1925 when not travelling around the world.

Aggrey was not only charming and saintly; he was a man of

great intelligence and capacity, yet at this distance of time he seems a little too deferential in his acceptance of European standards and leadership. It cannot be gainsaid that by the 1920s (and indeed in many places for long years before) there was a large tension growing between white control and African initiative, a tension which was one of the leading factors in the creation of independent African churches. The movement to break away from white control and establish purely African churches had begun in the last years of the 19th century in the two areas where Christianity had developed most strongly—South Africa and Nigeria. By 1920 there were 90,000 adherents of independent churches in the latter country and more in the former. In the following years more and more churches were to develop both there and elsewhere. Some of the new churches, particularly the early ones, adopted the exact pattern of liturgy, doctrine and ministry which had been experienced in a parent mission; but others, originating not from the break within a community but from a single prophetic figure and the clientele which congregated around him, developed a far more original pattern of life emphasising aspects of religion and human need, particularly healing through prayer, which most mission churches had appeared to ignore. They were black churches for black people where black men could come to the top, but they were seldom anti-white, and they often preached to people who could never have been reached by a mission church anyway. While some (though not all) accepted sides of traditional life, such as polygamy, which had been strongly condemned by the missionaries, it is not true that in general they were notably syncretistic or easily tolerant of traditional African religion. On the contrary, the prophets and preachers of independent churches have at times adopted a more vigorously hostile line to 'fetishes', shrines and 'pagan' worship than the missionaries themselves. But, above all, where the mission churches tended to be increasingly concerned with institutions, the independents have made of prayer, healing, and a very simple evangelical preaching the centre of their religious life.

Frequently the prophets did not themselves intend to found a new church but invigorate or extend an existing one; it was rather the refusal of church authorities to find room for this unexpected assistance which drove new groups into ecclesiastical independence just as it had driven Wesley in the 18th-century Church of England. The greatest prophets intuitively sensed the underlying needs of ordinary people in a time of major social uncertainty and stress—

in the years of establishment of foreign rule, war, or epidemic, new pressures were greatly increasing the worries that people felt and which could no longer be dealt with by the traditional means. There was more fear of witchcraft in many places, not less. The phenomenal success which some of the prophets have had must then be related not only to the undoubted spiritual power of particular individuals but also the circumstances of the moment.

Perhaps the most remarkable figure of all was that of the Liberian William Wade Harris. The 'Prophet Harris' as he was generally known (but he was apparently called 'Professor Harris' in the western Gold Coast) has become a figure of legend but his recorded achievement was singular enough. He himself founded no church, ordering people to go to the churches of the missionaries, Protestant or Catholic, or—if there were no missionaries around— to await their arrival with the Bible. It does not appear that he read his Bible to people, perhaps because his own education was extremely limited, but it was without doubt the central symbol of his work and its veneration the enduring mark of the congregations which arose from his preaching. 'God has sent me to burn the fetishes' he proclaimed, and the fetishes were burnt by the hundred. 'Are you the great spirit of whom they speak?' the people asked him. 'No' he replied, 'I am a man coming in the name of God, and I am going to baptise you in the name of the Father, Son and Holy Ghost—and you will be a people of God.' He was wholly self-assured, simple in his message, frequently irate and overbearing in his conduct, yet immensely persevering in response to the needs of endless people. With his cross, his Bible and his bowl for baptism in hand, he walked and preached along the west African coast from Liberia, through the Ivory Coast, into the Gold Coast and then back to Ivory Coast from 1913 to 1915 in the most extraordinarily successful one man evangelical crusade that Africa has ever known. Everywhere the people flocked to him, evil spirits were cast out, tens of thousands were baptised, fetishes were ruthlessly destroyed and Sunday was henceforth dutifully observed as a day of religious rest.

The French colonial administration in the Ivory Coast where he made his greatest mark was initially delighted with the effect of his preaching: if Sunday was now observed as a day of rest, people worked harder than before on the other six, moreover Harris preached obedience to colonial authority. However, it soon appeared to the authorities that the whole thing was getting out of hand and Harris was expelled. Yet, despite the government's subsequent attempt to suppress the whole movement, the religious beliefs of the coastal people had been permanently changed in those few months and the Bible (generally the English Authorised Version of which next to no one could understand a word) had become the most prized religious symbol in scores of villages. For years they awaited the white missionaries whom Harris had promised, but it was not until 1924 that the Methodist Church suddenly discovered that tens of thousands of unattached Christians were apparently quietly waiting for someone to come and instruct them. Catholic missionaries in the Ivory Coast had had little success on account of their rigid ways and failure to respond to the Bible symbol. In the meantime a characteristic pattern of church life had inevitably developed among the Harrisists, each congregation being led by Twelve Apostles as elders, and while many thousands willingly entered the Methodist Church in the 1920s, many others were unwilling to do so and finally established a fully independent church, the *Eglise Harrisiste*.

Only six years later a still more famous figure appeared in the western Congo: Simon Kimbangu. His likeness to Harris is in many ways remarkable. A Baptist by background, he felt called by the voice of Christ in 1921, when in his early thirties, to preach the gospel of the one God, in whom alone one must trust, and to heal the sick. Fetishes must be cast firmly aside. The fame of his healing was quickly such that missions and hospitals for miles around were almost deserted while all the world hurried to Simon's village of N'Kamba. The reaction of missionaries—Catholic missionaries above all—and of the Belgian colonial authorities was rapid and unfavourable. Simon was arrested and brought to trial for subversion in October 1921 with several of his apostles. 'Are you the prophet?' the judge asked him and he answered 'Yes'. He was sentenced to one hundred and twenty lashes to be followed by execution—a man whose dignity of bearing at the trial was outstanding and of whom it could not be shown that he had actually caused, or intended, harm to anyone. The King of the Belgians commuted the death sentence; Kimbangu was flogged and sent far away to lifelong imprisonment in Elizabethville. He died there, still in prison, in October 1951.

Kimbangu's public ministry had lasted only five months, yet his name has remained dominant in Zairean religion from that time to this. Attempt after attempt was made to stamp out his influence but in vain. The long effort of suppression is still more strange if one remembers how very straightforward his teaching was. There is no evidence that it had any explicit political reference. His doctrine had an extremely ascetic moral character and, unlike most African prophets, he had even condemned polygamy. As with Harris so with Kimbangu—there is no evidence that he intended to found a new church but this again is what happened when, in the 1950s, the persecution finally ceased. Kimbanguists found that they were not welcome in any of the existing churches and today 'the Church of Jesus Christ on earth through the Prophet Simon Kimbangu' is the second largest in Zaire and present in several other countries too. It is directed by Kimbangu's youngest son, Joseph Diangienda.

In British Africa the government had been far less averse to prophets and their churches. In South Africa they were already numerous. In the Gold Coast the Musama Disco Christo Church (the army of the Cross of Christ) was founded by the prophet Jemisimiham Jehu-Appiah in October 1922. In Nigeria 1925 was to prove a memorable year. On 17 May a young Anglican catechist, Josiah Oshitelu, had a vision of a large eye 'reflecting as a great orbit of the sun' and from June on he began to fast and record in notebooks a series of voices. Over the following years he was to fill six massive journals with these revelations. That same June, the 18th, the feast of Corpus Christi, again in western Nigeria, a fifteen-year-old girl, Abiodun Akinsowon, went with her two cousins to watch the annual Corpus Christi procession in Lagos. Beneath the canopy by the host she saw an angel who followed her home where she fell into a trance. From it she was recalled by a well known man of prayer, Moses Orimolade. From the spiritual partnership then established the 'Seraphim Society' was born that September, to become two years later the 'Cherubim and Seraphim', just as from the ecstatic experiences of Oshitelu would develop 'the Church of the Lord'. This then was the moment that *Aladura*, the praying churches of Nigeria, were about to break forth, though neither Moses Orimolade nor 'Captain' Abiodun nor Josiah Oshitelu intended in 1925 to found a new church. Aladura began in the form of religious societies within the existing churches but here as elsewhere the tension between new and old proved too great; their special claim to authority brought criticism and condemnation, and little by little they issued forth as separate ecclesiastical entities. All over Nigeria in September 1975 Cherubim and Seraphim were celebrating their golden jubilee, one among the multitude of churches of prayer, fasting and spiritual healing which have grown up in Africa.

By 1975 African Christianity was looking very different from how it had looked in 1925. First of all, the political situation has again changed radically. The colonial system so very settled in 1925 has now almost everywhere faded away. The young men and women of Nigeria or Zaire can hardly remember a time when their country was not independent. The five million Christians of 1925 are now some ninety million. The number of churches, dioceses, missions, even foreign missionaries has all vastly grown. Even if the missionary force has somewhat decreased since 1965, it is still more than three times as numerous as it was in 1925—40,000 in place of 12,000.

In the 1920s there was everywhere something of a surface calm, though the emergence of so many prophetic figures at that time and the great welcome they received suggest that, in the souls of many, things were far from tranquil: there was already a deep conflict between two patterns of life, old and new, within which ordinary Africans found themselves torn apart. Fifty years later all the tension has come to the surface. Political independence has proved the arena for the reassertion both of new and old. The formal eradication of colonialism has been in truth the takeover of the European system substantially unchanged by an élite trained in a European way to run a European conceived government, economy and educational system. In a sense the recipe of post-independence Africa has been no more complex than 'the same but more of it'. On the other side the slogans of independence have proved the stimulus for a collective re-examination of the pre-suppositions of society and its sense of direction. This critique is not one that can be carried on in tranquillity. The pressures of the population explosion, poverty, rapid urbanisation, the breakdown of that very machinery of government which the new élite inherited from the colonial powers, all this has created such a crisis of society that even a hardened well-wisher can ask despairingly 'Can Africa survive?'

The churches are caught up in every side of the tension. They may as well be rejected by the Marxist innovator as by the traditionalist insisting upon African 'authenticity'. They may be identified with the privileged rich élite, with patterns of neo-colonialism, but also with the under-privileged masses struggling for freedom, regional autonomy or simply protesting against the corruption of their masters. Nearly all of them are, far more clearly than in earlier decades, African churches. Almost all the leaders of the mission-connected churches are now African, the remaining missionaries playing in most places an increasingly subsidiary role. From this point of view the gap between 'mission churches' and 'independent' churches has diminished. But this does not mean that the mission-linked churches can now always brush off the charge of being an alien element without difficulty. Much about them remains undoubtedly alien, even unnecessarily alien. Yet so is very much else in modern Africa, and inevitably. The character of the churches and their leadership often harmonise only too well with the wider character of contemporary society and the leadership in other areas of life.

The political, intellectual and business leaders of today's Africa have come largely from the same stable. They too are mostly Christians, except in the predominantly Moslem areas; they went through the church schools and are aften closely linked by blood or friendship with the ecclesiastical leaders. Senghor studied in a seminary; Kaunda's father was a Presbyterian minister; Kenyatta's brother-in-law is a priest; Muzorewa is a Methodist bishop, Sithole a Methodist minister and Nkomo a Methodist lay reader. Nyerere likes nothing more than to sit down and argue things out with a bench of bishops. The Church's fate and public image depend as much upon these men as upon the purely ecclesiastical leadership.

The churches could not possibly remain uninvolved in the spate of political conflicts which have swept across Africa—their members are fully caught up in them and generally on more than one side. Christians were profoundly committed to either party in the Nigerian civil war; they provided the greater part of the southern leadership in the Sudanese civil war; they were predominant among both Batutsi and Bahutu in the bitter tribal conflicts of Burundi and Rwanda; they have taken every point of view in regard to the racial conflicts of the south. Cardinal Malula had to go into temporary exile after challenging President Mobutu at the start of the 'authenticity' campaign, while elsewhere in many countries bishops, priests and numerous members of their congregations have been imprisoned, exiled and killed.

Three Christians murdered in 1972 may stand for the many who have suffered in the conflicts of this period. Father Michel Kayoya was a brilliant young Hutu priest in Burundi, the author of two very beautiful books, *My Father's Footprints* and *Between Two Worlds*, in which he discussed the relations between African tradition, humanism, Marxism and Christianity, and criticised the craving for money, social parasitism and legal insecurity of modern Burundi. In the wake of the Hutu rebellion he was arrested and shot without trial on 17 May at a bridge over the Ruvubu river. He was buried in a common grave with some seven thousand other victims.

In September the Chief Justice of Uganda, Benedicto Kiwanuka, was suddenly seized and never seen in public again. Benedicto was a devout Catholic and a good family man, a lawyer of integrity and the country's first prime minister. He had been in prison for years under Amin's predecessor Obote, was released by Amin, made chief justice but had then courageously used his position to temper his country's increasingly illegal and bloodthirsty tyranny. He paid the price of a terrible death, being dismembered alive in the military prison of Makindye. He was only one, if the most distinguished, among thousands of victims.

In June 1972 a large number of Protestant church leaders in Mozambique were suddenly arrested by the dreaded Portuguese political police, the DGS, and imprisoned in the concentration camp of Machava. Among them was Zedequias Manganhela, president of the Presbyterian synodal council, an elderly pastor, a family man in his sixties. In the subsequent months he and his fellows were ruthlessly interrogated day after day in the attempt to establish links between the protestant churches and Frelimo. Then one morning, 11 December, Manganhela was found hanged in his prison cell, again one victim among very many of the racial tyranny and police brutality of southern Africa.

Kiwanuka the lawyer and politician, Kayoya the brilliant young priest author, Manganhela the quiet humorous old pastor—these can stand for many, victims of black oppression as well as white, tribal and racial conflict, man's inhumanity to man. Nevertheless the dominant impression of these years is not one of persecution and martyrdom. It is rather one of growth, success, increasing self-confidence, and often rather friendly relations between church and state. Twenty-five years ago, in 1950, some people were asking themselves what would happen to the churches in Africa once European rule was brought to an end. Clearly the churches came to most parts of the continent within the wider context of colonial expansion: the two movements were often closely linked. There was no alternative. But if that was so, might not the two end together as well? Or, at least, would not the churches greatly decline once African political independence was achieved? It can now be seen that such questions derived from a deep misunderstanding of the depth to which Africans both in the 'mission' and in the 'independent' churches had made Christianity their own. In fact, all in all, the post-independence years have been ones of an almost spectacular ecclesiastical advance.

The problems of the Christian churches in Africa today are many and deep; but they are seldom problems of decline. They arise instead from the sheer rapidity of growth, from an almost discordant vitality, from the need and often too the determination to reshape the pattern of church life and thought learnt from European missionaries, directly or indirectly, to accord with the complex religious and secular needs of African society, while remaining faithful to the essentials of Christian tradition. While many of the problems are ones which in some way or other affect other parts of the world church, their specifically African character remains very strong and it is as such that we want to understand them. In the following chapters we will look at some of those issues with which the African church is having today to wrestle most earnestly: ministry, structures, the role of foreign missionaries and financial self-reliance; culture and identity; sickness and spiritual healing; politics, poverty and power.

CHAPTER 2

Ministries, missionaries and moratorium

In May 1974 the third assembly of the AACC, the All Africa Conference of Churches, met in Lusaka, bringing together representatives of 112 member churches, including the Orthodox Church of Ethiopia, the Kimbanguists and two or three other independent churches; the assembly included official Roman Catholic observers and other visitors, but the vast majority of independent churches and some more isolationist Protestant mission-connected bodies were not represented. The first assembly had been held eleven years before, 1963, in Kampala, though there had been a preparatory conference in Ibadan in 1958, and the second assembly was at Abidjan in 1969. For ten days hundreds of Christian leaders from Madagascar to Senegal, from the Sudan to South Africa met to discuss and give witness to their faith in Christ and its implications for every side of human life.

In the Catholic Church too there have been major panafrican gatherings in the last twelve years of which the best known was that in Kampala in 1969 when Pope Paul visited Africa to lay the foundation stone for the new shrine of the Uganda Martyrs at Namugongo and to attend the inaugural meeting of SECAM, a body linking for the first time all the Catholic bishops of Africa. Prestigious meetings of this sort now draw church leaders together every year or two at very considerable expense to discuss matters of common concern and issue statements. Such gatherings are reported in the world press and they somehow symbolise the growing self-consciousness, the sense of shared identity, which African Christians have come to feel despite the deep divisions of denomination, country and language. Their decisions and declarations may have little lasting significance but they are celebrations of unity, of a common faith and commitment within a sea of diversity—a diversity which, for the rest of the time, is immensely appreciated.

In Europe and North America there is nowadays very

frequently a slight sense of shame about Christian denominational divisions. This is seldom to be met with in Africa. In Zaire a united Protestant Church (excluding only the Kimbanguists) has indeed come into existence on African initiative with considerable speed—but it has been at the behest of President Mobutu, impatient with a multiplicity of ecclesiastical bodies just as his ally President Amin was impatient with conflict inside the Ugandan Anglican Communion. Elsewhere unity schemes, whether they have succeeded (as, in the early 1960s, in the case of the United Church of Zambia) or whether they have finally come to little (as in the case of Nigeria or East Africa) have almost invariably been the brainchild of Protestant European missionaries anxious to apply a model which their counterparts adopted with success in India and which has also been canvassed with some success in the home churches of Britain and North America. They blame themselves that they (or rather their predecessors) brought to Africa denominational divisions; now, before leaving, they must heal these mission-imported schisms, establishing instead 'organic unity'—at least between such groups as Congregationalists, Presbyterians, Methodists and Anglicans. They are operating here according to the western Protestant ecumenical orthodoxy fashionable from the 1930s to the 1960s. But Africans seldom see things the same way. They may be willing enough on occasion to castigate the missionaries for introducing so many different churches, each representative of one segment of European ecclesiastical history, but—deep in their hearts—they take a real delight in all this variety to which, as we have already seen, they have added a great many extra brands of their own. At an ecumenical meeting in Zambia several years after the inauguration of the the United Church one of its members, a devout lady working full time for an important church sponsored project, expressed her views about unity: 'I was born a Methodist' she said, 'and I will die a Methodist.' She did not reject the United Church, she saw its practical point, but it had certainly not fired her imagination.

This does not mean that the ecumenical movement does not exist among Africans; simply that it is taking a shape of its own. There is the greatest pleasure in recognising the wider Christian fellowship and in occasional participation in celibratory gatherings such as those of the AACC. There is also a great deal of practical co-operation at national level, for example in theological training. Such things may come more easily than in Europe. The splendid development of Multimedia Zambia (founded in 1970) is another case in point—a joint initiative of Roman Catholics and of the Zambia Christian Council, comprising fourteen member churches. This has resulted in a fully integrated approach to radio and TV, the press and book publication. It produces its own monthly paper, the *Mirror*, while its book department brought out forty titles in the first three years. But here too it must be said that this has been a predominantly expatriate initiative. A strength of such schemes is that they are primarily related to the administrative and semi-secular sectors of church interest. They do not attempt to dominate or unify the field of worship.

The normal pattern of worship, belief, evangelism and pastoral care remains in Africa uninhibitedly denominational. Only in very few places would Christians of different churches want to share regularly at this level. The denominational tag— whether originating in Europe or in Africa, whether it be Lutheran or Kimbanguist—is not something about which people feel a little ashamed, but rather something to glory in. Undoubtedly many African Christians do greatly value a communion which extends far wider than their local church, but they find it already existing within their denominations. The Anglican communion may, as such, be fading away in Asia, it is doing no such thing in Africa, where Christians of this tradition rejoice in their particular link with Canterbury. Catholics especially—and about half all African Christians are after all Roman Catholics—immensely value the international bonds and full fellowship which are so strong a feature of their communion together with the many services which Rome provides, even if they can also be highly critical of Roman control. They are entering more and more actively into the debates of the Roman synod of bishops and into such other activities as that of the Association for the Propagation of the Faith, the chief Catholic international funding body which collects money all over the world to be allocated by a council consisting of representatives of all the churches concerned. If today the annual allocations are made principally to Africa and Asia, a hundred years ago they went to the United States and Great Britain.

Christian churches are societies of people involving structures and organisation at a variety of levels—local, regional or diocesan, national, international. There are bishops and archbishops, synods and their presidents; there are also the managers of schools and hospitals as well as their teachers, nurses and doctors; there are theological colleges and specialist agencies such as literature bureaus. Most important of all, there are the basic local needs to meet: common prayer and sacrament; preaching and teaching—especially of children and new members; regular pastoral care. How is all this catered for on a continuing basis in the length and breadth of Africa?

Throughout Africa, as throughout the world, most Christians take it for granted that Christian life means being a member of a local congregation—the Christians of your own denomination in a given locality who will worship together in a building set aside for the purpose. They tend to take it for granted too that the congregation will be linked with or responsible for various other activities of a more or less secular kind—a primary school, womens' clubs, a dispensary, outings of one sort or another. They assume too that a congregation should have a 'minister' of its own or at least share one with one or more neighbouring congregations. The minister's qualifications may be years of training in a college or they may be recognised experience or manifest charismatic power. His duties will consist in the leadership of worship, in teaching, in some pastoral care, and possibly too in the guidance or supervision of some of the more secular activities in which his congregation is interested. Almost all churches recognise a hierarchy of ministers with greater or lesser authority, ordained or unordained, but some tie this much more closely than do others to a period of formal training. All churches have to face the very considerable problem in very poor countries of financial support, but patterns here vary greatly. Some regard the norm as the 'full time' minister financially supported by the church, others take this to be the exception, even a very rare exception. In general the higher anyone is within his church's hierarchy the more likely it is that he is financially supported by the church; the lower he is—that is to say, the more he is the immediate and regular minister of a local congregation, the more likely it is that he has to support himself as any other working man.

If there are 90 million Christians in Africa today, probably at least 75 million of them are in the mission-connected churches. Fifteen years ago, in 1960, the figure was well under forty million, and thirty years ago, 1945, under twenty million. Such a vast and rapid growth in church members requires too a very great increase in the number of ministers and in the wider fabric of ecclesiastical structure. But this has proved far more difficult to bring about than the instruction and baptising of neophytes and infants. This is partly because the training of a professional clergy (and basically nearly all the mission churches thought of the clergy in a fairly professional way) on a large scale not only involves a good deal of time (including a course of probably at least three years) but also a great deal of money and of skilled personnel to staff the training colleges. But it was partly too because even at the close of the 1950s church leadership in many places was still remarkably cautious, and even hesitant, about the training of African ministers; partly because they did not for long grasp how great the growth in church membership was now proving to be.

There has been a very marked expansion of ministerial training throughout Africa in the last fifteen years, yet this has still fallen far short of what appears needed. Almost everywhere the churches remain very short of clergy, but this very scarcity of the traditional type of minister has helped to force them into new patterns of ministry and congregational responsibility which may prove far more creative than the careful extension in 20th-century Africa of a system of seminary trained clergy which was, after all, evolved for the most part only in 19th-century Europe.

Until the last few years the mission churches counted in Africa upon an ever increasing number of foreign missionaries. If in 1925 there were 12,000, today there are about 40,000, despite some decline since 1965. Of course not nearly all of these are ordained ministers. About a quarter, indeed, are religious sisters, mostly occupied in hospitals and schools. However, the number within the narrower ministry of the church—evangelical and pastoral— certainly remains very considerable, at least within the Roman Catholic Church. If the total number is now falling, and it is, this is by no means so fast a process as some may imagine. It is true that the main line Protestant churches (Lutheran, Anglican, Methodist, and Presbyterian) have considerably decreased their missionary personnel in these years, and so have some Roman Catholic societies. On the other hand some fundamentalist Protestant missions have actually increased at the same time, and so have certain other Catholic orders. In some cases new groups, not previously working in Africa, have entered since independence. It is to be noticed that missionaries, especially new missionaries, tend to be concentrating on certain countries and withdrawing from others either by necessity or persuasion.

What is undeniable is that by and large missionaries today are no longer central to the Christian situation of Africa, despite their continued presence in sizeable numbers. Their overall impact is steadily decreasing and, of course, a very considerable proportion among them are decidedly elderly. This does not mean that many are not doing excellent work or that in some places (particularly within a number of Roman Catholic dioceses) they do not continue to control the local church. But essentially their day is past. Their presence can now be an embarrassment and even, at least in some circumstances, a disservice to the cause of African Christianity. While they cannot solve the problems of the African Church they can defer a solution to those problems—sometimes by usefully giving the local leaders a breathing space, but often by providing a sense of false security and by at least implicitly upholding a misplaced model of church life. Their existence in relatively large numbers can easily suggest that the Church in Africa is more foreign than it really is and thus provide unnecessary ammunition for its critics. Whatever the intentions of individuals, the legacy of a recent colonial past and the continuing reality of neocolonialism in other fields can ensure that the presence of dozens of Americans or Irishmen in a church facing the contemporary storm of nationalism and cultural revolution is a source of weakness, not of strength.

These and other considerations explain why in the last few years there has been a growing call for a missionary 'moratorium': the proposal that no more missionaries and no more money be sent from outside to the African church for a certain number of years. The appeal for this was voiced very powerfully in 1971 by John Gatu, now chairman of the Presbyterian Church in Kenya, in a speech in Missouri which aroused the consternation of North American missionary circles. This was followed up by the AACC Assembly at Lusaka in 1974:

'To enable the African Church to achieve the power of becoming a true instrument of liberating and reconciling the African people, as well as finding solutions to economic and social dependency, our option as a matter of policy has to be a Moratorium on external assistance in money and personnel. We recommend this option as the only potent means of becoming truly and authentically ourselves while remaining a respected and responsible part of the Universal Church.

'The call for a Moratorium may undoubtedly affect the structures and programmes of many of our churches today. But a halt to receiving financial and human resources from abroad will necessitate the emergence of structures that would be viably African and programmes and projects of more urgent and immediate priority. A moratorium on funds and personnel from abroad will also enforce the unifying drive of Churches in Africa.'

Despite outward agreement at Lusaka on the principle, there is no real agreement either as to its meaning or as to its desirability. Some of those who urge it see the policy as being an essentially temporary one, to enable the churches in Africa to readjust better to the new cultural situation; others, and especially Canon Burgess Carr, the Liberian General Secretary of the AACC and the strongest proponent of the policy, see it as more than a moratorium, as a permanent full stop. For Carr the end in view is 'to stop overseas aid. Period. Forever.' Yet it has to be said at once that the complexities of the situation are such that at the same time the AACC itself has launched a larger appeal than any other ecclesiastical body in Africa for overseas funds—to build its new headquarters in Nairobi.

While almost all church leaders are agreed that the church should be more self-reliant than it is now, very many are also anxious to go on receiving some overseas help: they are only too conscious of the limitation of their own resources and the great calls that are made upon them. When governments and other secular organisations receive considerable foreign assistance in money and expert personnel, it seems madness to many that the churches alone should totally renounce such help. For such people the missionary contribution to the African church is already diminishing fast enough—fewer and fewer people volunteer in Europe and North America for missionary work, while world inflation is severely cutting ecclesiastical financial resources almost everywhere. Such processes may need little theoretical encouragement to achieve a large measure of practical 'moratorium'. As a matter of fact, the churches and missionary societies abroad which have paid most attention to the moratorium appeal are precisely those bodies whose commitment to missionary work is anyway seriously diminishing. The more 'conservative' bodies (Evangelical or Catholic) whose commitment has not changed tend to reject the appeal out of hand as theologically unjustified: the obligation to preach the gospel is an absolute one which cannot be abandoned on any grounds. In practice the issue is such a complex one, so variously seen by different churches and in different countries, that it can best be related to a variety of particular ecclesiastical situations.

Side by side with the mission-founded churches, others have been growing up independently, as we have seen, under African inspiration in many parts of the continent. We must now look at these churches more closely, while noting at once that they are bodies to whom the moratorium debate hardly applies: their help from abroad has always been either nil or very slight. They are most numerous in South Africa, Rhodesia, Kenya, Zaire, Nigeria and Ghana, but are numerous all along the west African coast from Sierra Leone to Calabar. In some countries, on the other hand, they have hardly developed at all and in a few, while they were significant fifty years ago, they have since diminished to form only a very small section of the total Christian community. Such countries are Tanzania, Uganda, Rwanda, Burundi, Malawi, Cameroon. Clearly these are some of the most important countries of Christian Africa and any adequate consideration of this subject must bear in mind the remarkable absence of independence in Tanzania as much as its remarkable growth in Nigeria. While in some countries, notably South Africa and Nigeria, the most important independent churches emerged fifty years ago or more, in others, such as Kenya and Ghana, they are mostly of more recent origin. Indeed in Ghana in 1960 these churches were still rather few and small; fifteen years later they have vastly multiplied and it is at least possible that they will do the same at some future date in countries where they at present hardly exist.

Such a rich and varied movement cannot be explained, still less explained away, in terms of just one or two causes. There are undoubtedly certain major secular contributory factors of which racial discrimination has been, perhaps, the chief: racial discrimination not only in society at large but also inside the church and inside the church's ministry. It could be a decisive factor, even in countries where the wider social discrimination seems of marginal importance, if it controlled the pattern of clerical relationships and of promotion; if it made impossible the promotion of a black minister above a white one, however senior he might be in age or length of experience. Three of the chief areas of separatism have been South Africa, Rhodesia and Kenya— three of the chief areas of white settlement and racial discrimination in Africa. There can be little doubt that the presence of a large body of white settlers and a discriminatory barrier in secular society, overwhelmingly accepted by white missionaries, had a profound effect on the whole temper of the mission churches in those countries, providing a grounding for ecclesiastical alienation: for that is what, from one point of view, independency has been— the spiritual alienation of Christians from the churches in which they first learnt of Christ. Such alienation was not, of course, limited to those countries but a comparable causality could be found elsewhere.

One must, however, probe further into specifically religious and ecclesiastical factors, often of a positive rather than negative nature. Such factors may be related either to the European or to the African contribution. On the European missionary side, there can be no question but that the vast majority of independent churches have grown out of Protestant rather than Catholic soil, and indeed out of certain Protestant strands rather than out of others. In the overall picture the *Maria Legio* of Kenya, with its strongly Catholic background, remains very much of an exception, though not unique. And even here it is fair to point out that it sprang forth in the early 1960s among a people, the Luo, in which other independent churches of a Protestant temper were already flourishing. The multiplication of churches is, after all, a striking characteristic of the historic Protestant tradition and it was exported to Africa as such: sometimes there were five or six different Protestant missionary groups at work within the same part of a single country and it does look as if it was in areas where the Protestant missionary tradition was most multiple that the African response to it was to produce with great gusto a new multiplicity. South Africa, western Kenya and western Nigeria are good examples. Such a response can be seen rather as one of creative fidelity to a tradition than as one of rejection of it. It has often been pointed out how many churches have come from Methodist missions, but 19th-century British Methodism with its frequent schisms surely itself provided the model. Why should the fissiparous process cease when the tradition is transplanted to Africa? New schisms can fairly be seen as showing that their African converts were good Methodists, rather than bad. If African Roman Catholics founded an independent church they were breaking with the primary tradition and the values their missionaries had stressed to a far greater extent than if African Methodists did so. All this is really to say that for the greater part African independent churches are clearly within the great tradition of Protestant Christianity and in these years this is being recognised more and more to be the case. Yet their pattern of growth, of authority and of ministry must be seen too as containing a strongly African contribution, sometimes a very original (or even an apparently 'catholicising') contribution, to this wider ecclesiastical stream.

This specifically African response depends for its content and stresses upon the African experience of religion prior to the coming of Christianity, upon the varying structures of local African society, and upon those contemporary human needs which the missionary churches have too largely ignored. While there was still some room for 'prophets' in the home churches of the missionaries, there was none for black prophets in the new churches they initiated, and yet the prophetic call was an important element in African traditional religions. Prophets had appeared in the past, particularly in circumstances of social stress, and new prophets appeared now within the Christian context. The missionary inability to contain them resulted almost inevitably in schism. Yet such prophets often sensed better than did the missionaries the most pressing human and spiritual problems facing ordinary people there and then—cultural alienation, the dislocation of family structure produced both by economic change and by the missionary rejection of polygamy, mental sickness, the fears related to witchcraft beliefs. To all these we will come back but the urgent need to wrestle with them—a need too often simply not recognised by missionaries—has provided much of the pressure behind the growth of the independent churches. The ministry of these churches has naturally developed on certain lines: while carrying across much of the freer Protestant tradition, it has had to subsist almost wholly without foreign money or formal theological training; it has been concerned very little with the institutional and educational administration which has taken up so much of the time of the ordained personnel within the mission churches; instead it has centred upon prayer and a direct personal and spiritual response to sickness, nervous breakdown and the resolution of private rather than public problems.

One of the most original 'ministries' which many independent churches have established is that of the 'holy city'—a religious and sacred centre where one can go on pilgrimage or even reside, be absorbed in lengthy and moving ceremonies of prayer, be healed of one's sicknesses. Such new Jerusalems now exist in many parts of Africa, from New Tadzewu in Ghana, the city of the Prophet Wovenu and the *Apostolic Revelation Society*, to Isaiah Shembe's Ekuphakameni in Natal, from N'Kamba-Jerusalem, Kimbangu's village in Zaire, to the Zion city of Bishop Mutendi by Mount Moriah in Rhodesia. Such cities have frequently a shrine in the centre in which the founder lies buried; they are hospitals in which people come for quite lengthy treatment, a sort of communal retreat and rest cure; they are monasteries—

permanent human communities specifically ordered according to a cycle of prayer and ritual. If the head of the Kimbanguist Church, Joseph Diangienda, is very much of a pastoral administrator, living in Kinshasa and visiting congregations up and down the country, in this conforming to the model of leadership of the older churches, his brother, Solomon Dialungana, is the custodian of the Holy Place and the writer of the church's doctrinal catechism. Resident in his father's village he represents a pattern of leadership to be found in many of the most thriving independent churches. In this as in many other ways the Kimbanguist 'Église' straddles old and new, two ecclesiastico-cultural streams. Certainly the holy city, its ministry both of healing and of pilgrimage, and the particular spirituality proper to an elect locality which develops across the liturgy of such a centre, all this provides what is one of the most characteristic features of the African independent church movement. The ancient Jewish love of Jerusalem manifested in so many of the psalms has been transformed in an excitingly creative manner, quite outside the patterns of missionary spirituality, to bring forth an enduring emotional force stretching beyond the lifetime or activity of even the most charismatic individual. In the words of one of the splendid Zulu hymns of Isaiah Shembe:

> I remember Ekuphakameni
> Where there is gathered
> The holy Church of the Nazarites.

> I remember Ekuphakameni
> Where the springs are
> Springs of living water, lasting for ever.

There are few major prophets in the African church today. The sons and disciples of a second generation have replaced them and preside over a steady round of prayer and healing, a more organised ministry, a greater concern for buildings and even in some cases the erection of denominational schools. The West African *Church of the Lord (Aladura)* had no schools for the first thirty years of its life from foundation in 1930. Today it has primary schools, a secondary boarding school and a theological seminary.

If there are some thousands of independent churches in Africa, the vast majority are extremely small, and many of these disappear after some years. Even such a great spiritual figure as the South African George Khambule who died in 1949 has now no church whatsoever to continue his tradition. A contrast needs to be made here between some forty churches which have continued to grow, some of them very remarkably in the last decade, establising in most cases a fairly regular organisational pattern and, on the other side, the many hundreds of very small groups, many of them never consisting of more than a single congregation with some score of members. There is a continuing emergence of new churches of this type, just as there is a continuing tendency for many to split up again and again or simply to disappear after a few years. A number of the larger churches, on the other hand, are now accepted members of local councils of churches; they co-operate in ecumenical ministerial training schemes; they may even receive a little financial help from abroad. In all these ways they approximate far more closely than formerly to many mission-connected bodies. Nevertheless they continue to show both greater flexibility and, on the whole, greater theoretical complexity in their ministry than the latter.

While the intricate hierarchy of *Maria Legio* in Kenya rising to pope and cardinals can be attributed to its Catholic background, churches stemming from Methodism may develop no less complicated a ministerial pyramid. The *Musama Disco Christo Church* in Ghana, for instance, has a dual ministerial structure, each with eleven grades, beneath its hereditary head prophet, the Akaboha. On the one side are the prophets, upon the other the pastors. Beneath the senior prophet and the regional prophet come prophets grade I to IV, non-grade prophets and junior prophets, beneath whom are three classes of healer. The pastors are similarly divided with below them classes of catechists and one of deacons and deaconesses. Lay office in the church is almost equally complicated, much of it being based on traditional Akan social structure, but the overall ministerial pattern is very similar to that of the mainly Nigerian Church of the Lord (Aladura).

This multiplication of ecclesiastical office contrasts strongly with the tendency to simplification and abolition of office observable in western churches today—where Roman Catholics have abolished most minor orders and the Church of England is considering the elimination even of the diaconate. But it should not be lightly concluded that this African tendency towards the refinement of hierarchy relating largely to ritual and vestment is necessarily counter-democratic; on the contrary, it could well be argued that the *ecclesia* can best realise *communitas* across the multiplication of roles even for fairly insignificant people whereby all are brought into the organic processes of the church, whereas an apparently democratic elimination of structure in fact leaves the church in the grip of a faceless bureaucracy. Hierarchy in an African church can be fully compatible with much discussion in council.

However extensive be the network of title and the development of ritual, the independent pattern of ministry remains overwhelmingly a self-reliant and untrained one geared either to a small but regular worshipping community or to a more transient clientele attracted by the possibilities of spiritual healing; though both of these are supplemented by the special facilities and ministry of a holy city of pilgrimage. The transient character both in attendance and in ministry in some churches is worth stressing; it is not accidental that in parts of West Africa these bodies are actually known as 'clinics'; in eastern Nigeria they are described as 'prayer houses', and their function may often be to supplement rather than wholly supplant the existing churches in a basically ecumenical manner. In fact many Christians take part regularly both in the services of a mission-connected church and of an independent 'prayer-house'.

The Protestant churches of mission origin have not hitherto demonstrated a comparable creativity, but they have greatly strengthened their ministry in the last fifteen years as well as vastly increasing the size of their membership. In some places, such as the Presbyterian or Methodist churches in Ghana, the process of establishing a full African leadership dates back many years, but it is surprising how few African ordained ministers other important churches had even in 1960, and at the highest levels of hierarchy they were still few and far between. At that time there was no single Anglican African diocesan bishop in east, central or southern Africa, though there were several in Nigeria. Well into the 1950s there was still not a single African member of the 'Congo Protestant Council' which represented most Protestant churches in that country and claimed to speak for at least a million Protestant Africans. The multiplication of ordinations and the transfer of leadership positions into African hands over the last fifteen years has been, in contrast, very marked. When the 1961 political crisis of Angola drove most of its Baptist population in the north into exile in neighbouring Zaire, they had not a single ordained minister among them. When fourteen years later, in 1975, the refugees returned *en masse* into Angola there were nearly forty ordained ministers to accompany them.

If the Anglican church in Uganda in 1960 formed part of the recently erected province of East Africa and consisted of two dioceses, each ruled by a white bishop with altogether two white and four black assistant bishops, today it is a province of its own with an archbishop and twelve diocesan bishops, all African.

The Evangelical Lutheran Church of Tanzania, one of the sturdiest Protestant churches in Africa, well illustrates the growth of these years. In 1955 it consisted of seven separate churches, all headed by foreign missionaries, with 206,000 baptised members. In 1959 the first African president was elected—for the northern district. By 1965 there were 413,000 members and in 1975 673,000 in eleven dioceses or synods, all now headed by Tanzanians. There are some four hundred pastors but there are still well over one hundred foreign missionary assistants of various sorts. It is interesting to note that there is now a strong tendency towards replacing the title of 'superintendent' or 'president' by that of 'bishop': there are already four bishops in the church and it may well be that this title will prevail everywhere in the future.

African Protestantism is tending towards episcopalianism, at least in title, despite the hostility to bishops of many of its founding bodies. If unity may be found in the office of bishop, it may also be found in the word 'Evangelical' which is becoming more and more the distinguishing name for African churches which have grown from the central Protestant tradition. It could well be that organic unity will finally thrive very much more under the flag of the deeply traditional Christian word 'Evangelical' than, for instance, under words such as 'United' or 'Ecumenical'. Its religious resonance is comparable with 'Catholic' and 'Apostolic'. These three words could well prove to be the best for labelling and identifying the three main Christian traditions in Africa.

The tendency within ecclesiastical government or organisation is everywhere towards a far larger number of units than those of colonial times. This responds not only to the overall growth of numbers but also to a markedly different pattern of church life, more reminiscent of the small diocese of the early church than of the large administrative unit of modern times. Diocesan administration is probably rather less stressed; the personal charisma of the bishop who is known to his own people becomes rather more important than formerly. The mission churches, both Catholic and Protestant, are here tending somewhat towards the pattern of ecclesiastical leadership to be found in the independent churches, just as the leaders in the latter have been moving to a certain extent in the direction of the former.

One of the most striking examples in the growth of hierarchy is that of the Methodist Church of Nigeria—one of the largest Methodist bodies in Africa. It has recently voted to accept not only priests and bishops but archbishops and a life patriarch. Here the traditional shape of western Methodist order would seem to have been completely overturned in a move towards the establishment of a complex hierarchy of authority comparable with that to be found both in the oldest churches of Christendom and in African independency. The overall movement is away from the rather egalitarian and externally democratic character of ministry stressed in modern western Protestantism.

Beneath the multiplication of hierarchical authority, however, the local congregation remains much as it ever was: the village fellowship with its small church, its catechist or reader, its praying core of men and women—women probably far more than men— very many of them permanently excluded from a rarely celebrated 'communion' because their marital status does not fit with church law; it is about as self-reliant and as self-ministering a model as any to be found in an 'independent' church. The moratorium debate does not affect the regular congregation of the Protestant mission-connected church any more than it affects an independent church because for many years now foreign missionaries and foreign money have hardly impinged at all at this level of church life.

The Roman Catholic position is rather different. Its scale is of course immense. It is present in all countries and is in many by far the largest Christian communion. In some it includes half or nearly half the total population. In all it has well over 300 dioceses in Africa and over forty million members. The debate over a Moratorium has been conducted almost entirely within Protestant churches but it might well be thought most relevant to Catholics for in Africa today there may still be some 25,000 Catholic missionaries—priests, sisters, brothers and lay people recruited explicitly by church organisations. While many of these are employed in schools, hospitals or various projects of secular development, the vast majority of the priests and very many of the sisters are primarily engaged in explicitly pastoral or evangelistic work.

While the large majority of bishops in independent Africa are now black, the large majority of priests (over 70%) remain white. At the same time the financial support provided from other parts of the Catholic world for African dioceses remains vast, though here again it reaches the administrative superstructure rather than the local congregations. While most Protestant churches in Africa have only a small, if significant, section of their ordained personnel and financial support from abroad, the Catholic Church as a whole could simply not continue functioning in its present form without such support. Nevertheless there are very considerable differences here. There are a fair minority of strong dioceses in which missionaries today play a relatively small part: such dioceses are to be found in central and western Uganda, in several areas of Tanzania; Rwanda and Burundi; Lesotho, the Igbo inhabited East Central State of Nigeria; southern Togo and southern Dahomey; north-western Ghana and the southern part of Upper Volta. There are no more than four thousand African priests today and over half of them work in fewer than fifty dioceses. These are the real strong points of African Catholicism while the other 250 odd dioceses have fewer than eight priests each and remain at present overwhelmingly dependent upon missionary societies despite a little assistance which the stronger dioceses are now offering to the weaker.

There are certain areas among the two hundred and fifty weaker dioceses which can only be classified as ecclesiastical disaster areas. Bad church policies in the past, large numbers of baptisms linked with an almost complete absence of local clergy and an unfavourable government have combined to produce a situation of manifest breakdown. Of these Angola and Mozambique are likely to be the most striking.

The giant within the Catholic Church in Africa remains Zaire claiming eight million or more members with 48 dioceses, but it is a giant with the most formidable of problems, still suffering the after effects of its highly privileged position in colonial times. Nowhere else (except in the Portuguese speaking territories) has such a deep psychological readjustment to the new Africa been required. In 1960 no country had more local priests and seminarians, but since then years of political disorder, followed by the cultural revolution and a long tussle with Mobutu, and the growth of the Kimbanguist Church have all left their mark. In the ten years from 1964 to 1973 182 new priests were ordained, an average of 18 a year which is hardly equal to one per diocese every three years, but here too most ordinations are for a small minority of the dioceses. Great cities like Kinshasa and Kisangani have a mere handful of local priests while in the new atmosphere of Mobutu's campaign for 'authenticity' foreign priests find it more and more irksome to continue working in the country.

Tanzania and Kenya illustrate the contrasts to be found within the Catholic Church today. Twenty of the twenty-four dioceses of Tanzania now have African bishops but still more significant is the overall strength of the local church, whether it be looked at in terms of lay organisations, sisters' congregations, the number of priests and seminarians. The Catholic strength is not by any means confined to a single party of the country but it has undoubted strongholds in four different areas—Bukoba in the north-west, Moshi in the north-east, Songea in the far south and Sumbawanga in the far west. The Catholic Church in Tanzania today, like the country itself, is tribally well balanced. There are now some six hundred African priests in the country and ordinations have reached an average of at least thirty a year. At the same time the number of missionaries—admittedly rather high in the past—is now falling fairly fast. In the six years, 1967–73, missionary priests decreased by 82, brothers by 70 and sisters by 64.

In the past the Catholic missionary commitment in Kenya was both smaller and less effective than in Tanzania. The training of local priests never got properly under way in colonial times and there are still no more than about one hundred today. Missionary personnel, on the other hand, has greatly increased since independence. In 1961 there were 415 expatriate priests, by 1973 there were 646. Kenya today seems to be Africa's haven for the foreign missionary though a rude awakening may well be on the way. It is, perhaps, not surprising that the call for a moratorium has come particularly strongly from some circles in Kenya, yet there are others, including Kenya's Cardinal Archbishop, who have called on the contrary for still more missionary help.

The shortage of African Catholic clergy almost everywhere is certainly connected with the continuing Catholic insistence upon a general law of clerical celibacy, though there has been far more to it than that. At the same time one must note a marked increase over the last eight years in the number of young men entering theological seminaries in many parts of Africa. If this is true for Protestants it is still more true for Catholics. The total number of Catholic seminarians was 1,661 in 1960, 1,924 in 1965, 2,562 in 1970, and 3,650 in 1975. Such a rise coming at a time when in most other continents the number of Catholic seminarians has steadily declined is very significant. It is true that for some years the actual number of ordinations did not rise, indeed there was an overall slump between 1967 and 1970. But the Catholic seminary training is a long one, normally six years, and the marked rise in seminarians only came after 1965. In 1973 ordinations rose well over 200 for the first time and this will surely be maintained. For a church of such a size, with over 300 dioceses to provide for and still growing fast all the time, that of course is by no means an adequate figure and in fact the rise comes chiefly in a few places, Nigeria especially and the East Central state of Nigeria above all. Nigeria had just 166 seminarians in 1960 and 196 in 1965. It was, strange as it may seem, with the civil war that this really changed. By 1970 there were 424 and in 1975 837. Of the 237 African secular priests ordained in 1973 84 were for Nigeria and 53 of those for the four dioceses of Onitsha, Owerri, Enugu and Umuahia. Igbo Catholicism is in this as in other ways atypical of Africa, but its sheer numerical weight is going to be a major force for the future.

The general picture of the Catholic Church remains an extraordinarily priestless one, indeed in most areas increasingly priestless, despite the theoretical dominance of priests within the Catholic structural pattern. Most African dioceses consist of some twenty 'parishes' staffed by one to three priests each, but each of these 'parishes' covers an enormous area of ground, scores of villages and probably at least twenty village churches many miles away from one another. As Bishop Kalilombe of Lilongwe in Malawi has remarked: 'Our system in the diocese as in practically all the sister dioceses around us, represents a sort of anomaly. We think and work in terms of "parish" and yet nobody is duped. In actual fact as far as real Christian life is concerned, it is on the sub-parish level that the real thing is going on.' That is where the true local church exists, the praying community which ought to be a eucharistic community but cannot be because it has no priest. Priests have never been able to visit the villages very frequently, but as the number of Christians has grown, personal contact between priest and people has declined still more. An increase in the number of African priests is balanced by a decrease in the number of missionary priests, but while the latter worked mostly in the countryside, the former tend to be placed far more in towns and specialist institutions. As a consequence, while village churches still multiply, the clergy concerned with them grows fewer and fewer.

Faced with this situation new forms of ministry, authorised and unauthorised, are appearing all across the continent: new schemes for training catechists, the granting of special powers to confer the sacraments both to catechists and to other lay leaders, new types of village team ministry, associations of women. Two points are becoming clear. The first is that the typical local Catholic pastor (at present not ordained) is likely to be married, a member of the local community, not too highly trained. His culture will relate to that of the community he lives in. The second is that he is likely to work with a church council of his own village or a group of villages, which will itself send representatives to a wider council for the whole area, at present the parish. The third is that a decisive factor behind the whole evolution of Catholic ministry is that of finance and the need to be self-reliant. Even if there were far more priests available of the traditional type, there simply would not be the money to support them in most parts of a very poor continent. The Catholic Church is slowly facing up to the problem, not of a viable system breaking down through a shortage of priests to run it, but of an unviable system requiring integral reshaping in the context of the wider society and its culture. The real pattern of worship, organisation and ministry already in operation in the villages owes remarkably little to immediately preceding European experience; it has been moulded by the inherent exigencies of the local situation and is not so markedly different from that existing either in Protestant mission-connected or in many of the independent churches.

At this level—the one really important one—the campaign for a moratorium is essentially an irrelevance. For many years now little in the way of foreign money or personnel has come through to the grass roots, though, admittedly, in the Catholic Church there are many dioceses where a white missionary continues to visit the villages from time to time, celebrate a solemn mass, take some decisions and offer pastoral advice. This is certainly still appreciated by many but its importance is rather marginal and in another five years time it will be a great deal more rare than it is today.

In the meantime missionary priests and outside money continue to provide a fair range of specialist services in a time of transition. Almost everywhere the call is now for self-reliance, though this call is taken a great deal more seriously by some people than by others. It cannot be questioned that the missionary era which began in the mid 19th century is now over and that a heavy foreign presence in African churches is increasingly inappropriate and can actually impede them from a full-hearted response to today's evangelical and pastoral challenges. On the other hand, outside the emergency of political compulsion, a sudden total withdrawal can seldom be justified and while being welcomed by some ecclesiastical intellectuals would be gravely misunderstood by the common man. African Christians have shown time and again a deep love for their missionaries, particularly for long term missionaries, and many ordinary people would neither understand nor forgive a hasty departure. Young and very poor churches continue to have a right to the support and co-operation of older churches, and it is absolutely proper that in a time of great growth, change and unanticipated challenges this support should continue to be forthcoming. It would be an eternal disgrace if the churches of the affluent west ceased at the present juncture to give financial support to their poorer brethren of the third world. The need of Africa today in the ecclesiastical as in the secular field is not for a hasty and ill-conceived moratorium but for a sensitive harmonisation of the claims of self-reliance with those for the expression and continuation of a wider human and catholic fellowship.

CHAPTER 3

Cultural revolution

In January 1972 a new law was promulgated in Zaire: Christian names were abolished forthwith. Only purely African names were henceforth to be used. It was part of the *kulturkampf* against the influence of the Christian churches which brought about, among much else, the temporary exile of Cardinal Malula of Kinshasa. But the decree was accepted: the well known priest, author and theologian Vincent Mulago became from that moment Mulago gwa Cikala Musharhamina, and with him all the millions of Christians in Zaire abandoned their baptismal names. This decree was the most striking expression yet of President Mobutu's policy of 'authenticity'—the assertion of African cultural values over against the European culture whose standards had been normative throughout the colonial period. 'Our ancestors never had such names' declared Mobutu: authentic African culture and authentic African names must now reappear from beneath that cultural imperialism of the west with which Christianity has, undoubtedly, been most closely linked. In other countries too, particularly Nigeria, some individual Christians have been abandoning their European names or, at least, refusing to have their children baptised with other than traditional African ones— generally names with deep religious meaning.

There can be no question but that Europeans in general and European missionaries in particular, with some few exceptions, admitted little if any culture of value in Africa, just as many had denied that it really had any religion—other than fearful superstitions. It was more or less taken for granted by many missionaries that the more a new social order, a new economy, a new culture, replaced the traditional one, the better for Christianity. African societies had a unitary cultural character, which does not mean they were static or uncomplicated or uniform. They were none of these things: their social, cultural and political institutions evolved; they frequently had a great structural complexity; they differed greatly one from another. But each one was all of a

37

piece, being permeated throughout by its own religious and moral values, even though there could also be a basic tension between different institutions within a single society, especially when those institutions derived from different epochs within that society's history. The predominating unitary character of such a society was not something special to Africa, though it was particularly marked here—perhaps because of a scarcity of religious or educational institutions or literature which clearly crossed political boundaries—but its inevitable consequence was that the things of religion were never clearly separable from the things of government, from daily life, from the civil ceremonies and social structuring of birth, marriage and death.

Many missionaries were extremely ignorant of the societies they had come to evangelise, with an ignorance partly blameworthy, partly next to inevitable. Moreover they came with an almost impregnable confidence in the overwhelming superiority of the European west and in all the ways of society and culture which they had taken for granted in their own homes, whether Evangelical or Catholic. Nevertheless a minority of missionaries proved themselves outstanding linguists and became deeply appreciative students of African custom. However, whether they were just plain ignorant or whether they were sensitive proto-anthropologists, their reaction over many matters did not vary greatly. This was partly due to the theological rigidity of almost all branches of the 19th- and early 20th-century church, but still more was it due to the intrinsic intertwining of religion and social life characteristic of traditional Africa.

There were early missionaries who encouraged the adoption not only of Christian names but of European family names as well —Dos Santos and Caetano, Johnson and Crowther; just as there were missionaries who absolutely condemned the payment of 'bridewealth' in marriage, all African dancing and participation in every traditional custom from cradle to grave. There were other missionaries who tried hard to distinguish in African culture between what was and what was not an apparently indissoluble part of African religion.

African culture was not, then, wholly condemned: polygamy was outlawed by almost all churches but, equally, bridewealth came to be allowed by almost all. The taking of European family names faded away when the missionaries moved inland from the coast and out from the 'mission villages' and small creole dominated port townships. The intensity of missionary influence decreased as the area subject to it vastly grew. A fusion began to establish itself, though more in practice than in theory. For the most part missionaries still found a vast range of African cultural practice incompatible with Christianity and taught accordingly. In school they were believed, at home very often they were not, and a type of institutional schizophrenia was built up between two overlapping comprehensive models of behaviour: one model, that of traditional African propriety, might justify and even require the exposure of twins; the other, that of missionary propriety, might condemn the chewing of cashew nuts. These are extreme cases; in between them there was and still is a vast range of cultural practice about much of which one can legitimately argue. A big middle ground was established, including such central social practices as plural marriage and the taking of title, rituals of puberty, of inheritance and so much else, which almost all missionaries for long judged negatively but which most African Christians long judged positively.

Deeper in its implications for common life than political imperialism was this basic and largely inescapable cultural imperialism implicit alike in missionary practice, in the development of formal education and in the establishment of a steadily expanding top rung of society ordered culturally on almost entirely western lines. Upon one side the pillars of traditional culture were dislodged or, at least, depreciated in significance; upon the other there was an imposition of new pillars—new standards of excellence, of wealth, of power, new forms of education, new loyalties. Most Africans, from chiefs to the poorest villagers, managed for many years to keep this totality of a new cultural universe at bay; they managed to marginalise it in regard to their own lives. Africa was too large, district commissioners and missionaries too few to break in overwhelmingly on most people's lives. A steady trickle of western ideas and artefacts remained small enough to be effectively absorbed into the traditional pattern. Elsewhere, in the environment of a town, a European owned plantation, a mission compound, a secondary school, the opposite appeared to happen: the new standards were publicly taken for granted, the traditional went underground. So little boys in French West Africa would even learn to say, unhesitatingly repeating their history text books, 'Our ancestors the Gauls', while little boys in British West Africa when asked to name their favourite song would as unhesitatingly reply 'The British Grenadiers'.

These were minority areas, but they were, of course, where the new men were being formed: the major innovating groups in society. The majority of this small minority seldom publicly challenged the new values. On the contrary their own status rather depended on upholding and propagating them. But a minority within the minority soon reacted differently and already before the end of the 19th century vigorously criticised this too obvious rejection of all things African, the elevation of all things European. Such a one was James Johnson, the Nigerian Anglican priest, who wrote in 1873: 'In the work of elevating Africans, foreign teachers have always proceeded with their work on the assumption that the Negro or the African is in every one of his normal susceptibilities an inferior race, and that it is needful in everything to give him a foreign model to copy; no account has been made of our peculiarities; our languages enriched with traditions of centuries; our parables, many of them the quintessence of family and national histories; our modes of thought, influenced more or less by local circumstances; our poetry . . .'.

Few men could express themselves with the clarity of James Johnson but his voice here represents the far wider movement of 'Ethiopianism', the assertion across the name of the continent's most famous kingdom, already to be discovered in the Bible, of the values of authentic African culture and history over and against indiscriminate Europeanisation. That Ethiopia was not only an ancient African kingdom but also an ancient Christian kingdom and church has been a point of immense importance in shaping both the aspirations of the independent church movement and those of cultural self-assertion by uniting the two under the banner of an ancient name as unquestionably African as it has been Christian.

The cultural conflict to which Johnson points has been carried on far less in print than in the hearts and life pattern of millions of mostly illiterate people, in a confused merging of values and aspirations, in the emergence of little oddly named sects up and down the continent. Essentially it has been the inevitable concomitant of a vast revolution in society and in the minds of men which has gone far beyond the fixed demands of civil government or the acceptance and rejection of credal formulas to affect every item of the common life style and draw into its vortex an ever larger proportion of the total population. Some even to this day have stood sturdily aside content with the ways of their ancestors; some have flung themselves in with never a word of regret; some have gone in far too far ever to return but have then bitterly condemned the cultural alienation they have experienced as the reverse side of the new education they have sought; many have established, almost unawares, something of a new status quo embracing in a manner more than syncretism and less than synthesis elements of the one tradition and of the other. So Senghor could already in the 1930s look back upon the village life of his childhood:

> I remember the funeral festivals
> steaming with the blood of slaughtered herds
> The quarrels, rhapsodies of the *griots*
> I remember pagan voices rhyming the Tantum Ergo
> and the processions and the palms and the arches of triumph.

Cultural enrichment; alienation; annihilation—how does one judge it? Modern Africa, freed from the immediate political yoke of Europe, is intensely conscious today of the cultural question. It knows as well as anyone that it may seem pretty inadequate, a piece of mere tokenism, even just silly, to reject a European name because one's ancestors did not have it, when one has no intention of rejecting the European motorcars and railways and aeroplanes, the telephone systems, the basic educational, economic and political structures which were all evolved in the west and transported to Africa during the colonial years. And yet, decisive as these things are, powerful as they have been in breaking down the old order and establishing a new, there is still an impersonal and almost non-cultural character to many of them which, as a consequence, does not wholly decide the shape and ethos of the more personal, artistic, ideological and religious spheres of life. One's name, after all, is the most precise assertion of one's identity— and the question of identity is what it's all finally about: who is one?

Comparably, the change of name of country which so many independent states have insisted upon is not a pointless exercise but rather a public announcement that at least in intention this society wants to be authentically itself, somehow profoundly continuous with its ancestry over the centuries; that this authenticity cannot be the same thing as mere continuity with the status established by even the most benevolent of colonial governors. A society has to find its own internal coherence and to adhere to and identify with certain mythical symbols, certain venerated founders. One and the same society can hardly be both 'Rhodesia' and 'Zimbabwe'—the points of reference of the two are utterly opposed. Yet Rhodesia exists and Zimbabwe does not, it may be replied, and even if Rhodesia is renamed Zimbabwe, it will continue to have the borders of Rhodesia and the capital of Rhodesia and the railways and road system of Rhodesia, all developed according to the ethos of Rhodesia as a follow-up to Rhodes' first column of pioneers—and all quite different from anything historically related to the culture and ruins of Great Zimbabwe. Yet the land remains the same, and the people remain predominantly the same, and the languages remain the same; the whole vast almost shapeless network of village communities remains essentially the same—the earth, the families, the languages that were there before Rhodes' men came north. The men of today cannot escape from the new political geography and all that goes with it, yet at the same time they want to reassert at surface level the still more important underlying values of popular continuity which have been ignored or greatly undervalued—seen simply as a *tabula rasa*, a mass of more or less compliant labour on which was to be built a new model. They want, then, to go back from being Rhodesia to being Zimbabwe, to shift their primary mythical collective symbol of identity from the grave of Rhodes in the Matopos Hills to the walls of the elliptical temple. They want, some more consciously than others, a cultural revolution beyond and below the political revolution.

A cultural revolution cannot but relate to the whole shape of the churches and of organised religion as much as to government or the life style of the individual. To the church, many would say, most of all: here was the most subtle and the most powerful source of cultural alienation. And not merely alienation, they would add, but annihilation. Despite the profoundly different approach of some enlightened missionaries, men like Father Aupiais in Dahomey and the Methodist Edwin Smith in central Africa, cultural annihilation is not too strong a phrase for what was attempted by many missionary groups and experienced at the receiving end by some Africans brought intimately within the ecclesiastical institution. A bright young man who had been taken into a minor seminary about the age of twelve for some six years there to be followed by another eight in a major seminary, during all of which he was systematically cut off from his own society, perhaps even forbidden to speak his own language, while he imbibed a formal education and way of life in no way different from that to be found in similar institutions in France or Ireland, could afterwards with full justification speak of the whole process as one of cultural annihilation. In the wider society, however, it may be questioned whether such a description is an apt one. Even if something of the sort was by some intended, the sheer vigour of modern African society has been such that it could not happen. African culture has not been annihilated, either inside the Christian churches or outside. The impact of those brief years of colonialism and missionary work was simply not sufficient. Nevertheless there has been a profound, and inevitable, sense of alienation, out of which has come all sorts of movements religious and political, including the present search for authenticity, a search sponsored alike by politicians and theologians.

It is a movement involving governments, intellectuals, the wider society; a search for meaning, for identity, for a culture which without fully repudiating the immediate past does justice to the roots of this society's being. In a real sense it is undoubtedly reactionary. In Chinese terms 'cultural revolution' has meant the sweeping away of tradition, of Confucius, of the whole weight of the historic past. In African terms 'cultural revolution' may mean today just the opposite. It means rediscovering the wisdom of the ancestors, revaluing their ceremonies, reawakening their names, renewing their languages. Of course a purely reactionary cultural revolution would be a flight from reality in present day Africa. For some that may indeed be the option they are really choosing, but not for most. On examination and despite the strong phrases, the 'authenticity' of Mobutu, for instance, proves to be but one aspect of a process of governmental modernisation in substantial continuity with the colonial past and the experience of autocratic centralised states in many parts of the world. The practice of Nyerere's socialism is very different from the traditional roots to which it appeals for justification. Today's authenticity in the secular order is not really the authenticity of the precolonial past. It could not be. Yet it may need the mythology of the latter to sustain the rigours of the former, to justify the harsh processes of government in a post-colonial world where political independence has not brought with it any great measure of prosperity for the masses of the people.

What of the Church? In no area, perhaps, has the cultural revolution been taken more seriously than in that of religion. This is partly because its critics and enemies, opposed to the undoubted influence the churches still have, perceive correctly that here can be found Christianity's Achilles heel in Africa—for all that it has done, does it not only too easily appear as a culturally alienating element? Still more, however, the pressure for cultural revolution in the religious field comes from committed Christians, conscious in themselves of the schizophrenia we have previously discussed and of the profound weakness this brings to church life. It is what the churches are themselves doing in this field that we must now consider.

The structural revolution of ministry and church government studied in the preceding chapter is itself, of course, part and a very important part of the church's cultural revolution. Culture implies the totality of social structure, art and artefact, language use, recreation, the intertwining of belief and life. Nothing that belongs to the regular pattern of life of an individual or a group is excludable from its particular cultural amalgam, though some things in it are more peripheral and transitory, some more basic and central. No group can conceivably change its deep religious beliefs and philosophy without noticeably changing its culture. Conversion to Christianity was bound to bring this with it. But just as after a religious conversion there is in reality a very considerable measure of continuity between the totality of the new religious beliefs and the old (the former can only be grasped and adopted by an individual or a group of people in terms of that which they already had, this being most true as an actual matter of vocabulary), so there is an immense measure of continuity between the culture of the preceding state and the culture of the subsequent.

At the moment of conversion one almost inevitably stresses the degree of rupture rather than the continuity involved in the process. This is likely to be psychologically necessary for the one undergoing the conversion: a new vision with new certainties and new duties includes the need for a discontinuation of many of the practices tied up in past experience with the old vision. At a later date the dimension of continuity will reassert itself: once one is surely established in the new fellowship one will bit by bit realise better the deep congruity of much that went before with one's present understanding. This is even more true of a new generation, people who never underwent personally the psychological trauma of the initial conversion nor experienced the old life as a social and spiritual unity. The African Christian baptised in childhood and educated in a Christian school may yearn to identify with ancestral spiritual roots and social practices in a way that a Christian who had once shared those roots and practices unselfconsciously but with all the constraints and inhibitions they carried with them, could never do.

All this is simply to say that there is a necessary dialectic in the conversion process which can only be worked out across the years. It is not to say that in many things missionaries did not go too far in stressing the initial rupture and in striving to create an almost total discontinuity between 'pagan' past and 'Christian' present.

One practice much discussed in West Africa, particularly Nigeria, is that of title taking. Social status depends to a great extent upon the acceptance of certain chiefly titles within a local community. The original duties, spiritual and material, related to these titles have largely passed away—just as in the British government titles like 'Lord Privy Seal' and 'Chancellor of the Duchy of Lancaster' remain in use though shorn of their initiating purpose—but the prestige belonging to them has not. Their bearers remain the natural leaders of the local community. It could be that a hundred years ago the ceremonies relating to such positions made it improper for any Christian to hold them and that missionaries were right to ban them, although it is more probable that in a time of conversion it is wiser to live with some ambiguity than to opt out of it compulsorily (unless an absolutely clear moral principle is at stake), but today it is undoubtedly better for Christians to take chieftaincy titles such as that of Ozo in Igboland. This indeed the Catholic Church there has now recognised.

More problematic, but no less important, is the issue of polygamy. Most African societies were traditionally fairly polygamous and of very many this remains true. It is not, of course, the case that all or most men have more than one wife, but many do—at least at some time in their lives, and in many places taking a second wife is generally regarded as a desirable thing to do. The immediate reasons for doing so may be many: the prestige of a chief or rich man, the barrenness of a first wife, the provision of help for a wife who is getting older and has to cope with a large family, the duty of providing for the widow of one's brother, additional labour in the family plantation, more sexual intercourse —particularly where the custom is for women to abstain from intercourse for a long period after childbirth. The list could be extended. Some reasons may seem more creditable than others, and some are falling into desuetude in a changing society. The modern widow may refuse point blank to be remarried to a brother-in-law, while in urban life a plurality of wives can prove an economic burden rather than a blessing. Even in Africa a multitude of children may no longer be sought after: it is better to have fewer children and educate them well than to have many and no money to pay their school fees. Many women, particularly those who have been to school, are now opposed to polygamy in a way they were not before: they are looking for a closer personal relationship with their husband than is practicable in a polygamous family. But here too there are vast differences between country and tribe. What is certain is that there are still millions of polygamous households in Africa, and that many of them are as stable and happy homes as the monogamous ones though their ethos be rather different. They include many Christians. In some countries at least 20% of all Christians are in polygamous marriages, an only slightly smaller proportion than that for the general population.

But almost all the churches have long banned polygamists, at least male polygamists, from communion and full membership. Are they right to do so? Is monogamy a matter of basic gospel morals about which the church cannot compromise or is it essentially a matter of culture and the varying family structure proper to a given economy or society? Or is it again a matter of the morally ideal, the preferable, the evangelical counsel of perfection—something like many other Christian ideals to be encouraged and preached about, but not something to be imposed on pain of excommunication.

There can be no doubt that by and large Christian missionaries in Africa in the 19th and 20th centuries have taken a very hard line against polygamy, despite the considerable doubts which a minority among them has always had and expressed about it. In practice, faced with a strongly polygamous society, they made of monogamy almost the touchstone of true Christianity—at least that is how it must have seemed to many Africans. And the refusal to baptise male polygamists could have much more cruel effects than the refusal of communion to a Christian taking a second wife, because in many cases the former brought about the breaking up of marriages and families entered into in all good faith in a fully responsible manner according to the only marriage law in existence in that society. Of course what the missionaries saw most forcibly were the many scores of wives which some chiefs had: if they allowed the commoner to keep his second wife, how could they have refused baptism to the king with fifty? Yet multiple polygamy of that sort entered into very often for political and prestigious reasons, seemed the very antithesis of the Christian ideal of marriage. As so often in real life every line of action was fraught with major moral inconveniences.

Should the churches today retreat from that position and be willing to receive polygamists to baptism? Should they even allow their members in some circumstances to take a second wife? No questions sustain more excitement within the church of Africa. Time and again in the last few years African theologians and some missionaries too have argued for a major change in church practice. The imposition of monogamy is seen as essentially an instance of western cultural imperialism condemning the marriage practices of Africa in favour of those traditional in Europe without any biblical warrant and indeed in contradiction to much Old Testament witness. But many other African churchmen and church women too reject any change equally fiercely. It is true that no word of the Bible certainly condemns polygamy and it is true as well that for the most part Christianity had spread elsewhere in the world among peoples already far more monogamous than were most African peoples. This, however, should not be pressed too much. There were many polygamous peoples in other parts of the world to whom the gospel was preached in the past, very notably the people of ancient Persia, a highly polygamous society. But nowhere did the church, so far as is known, modify its own insistence upon monogamy. New Testament marriage teaching does very clearly stress the essential reciprocity of the marriage covenant and it can well be claimed that such reciprocity is deeply violated by the right of a man to take more than one wife. The argument is not a simple one.

Is monogamy part of Christianity's own intrinsic authenticity or is it something very much less? Is polygamy part of Africa's perennial authenticity or is it, at least today, a marginal and socially retrograde phenomenon? If the churches alter their discipline now are they applying what was appropriate for yesterday's Africa to tomorrow's society? Will they be declaring 19th-century missionaries wrong at the expense of the rights of 20th-century African women? Would the church be giving way to male chauvinism yet again, sugaring it over with an appeal to culture? Or, on the contrary, will it be simply removing a mistaken legislation while allowing deeper movements to work their slow way to a more fully Christian society? Nowhere are issues more finely balanced, more complex, more open to firm yet contradictory

47

positions. On the whole pastoral practice here is softening and there is a fairly widespread tendency (following a decision by the Evangelical Lutheran Church in Liberia in 1951) to admit some long standing polygamists to full communion in certain conditions, but there is little sign of change in the overall insistence upon monogamy as a necessary characteristic of full Christian marriage.

Africa is a continent of song, dance and musical instruments. It is a continent of language and languages. Here lies the heart of its communal artistic inheritance and nothing was sadder than the missionary failure to open a door whereby at least some of this wealth might pass across into the worship of the young churches. The drum was not heard in most churches, only the harmonium accompanying carefully translated European hymns sung to the tunes of the west. The result was frequently deplorable; African languages could not be bent to European hymn tunes, although the Latin of the plainsong might enter in more deeply—mysteriously at home. Of course this missionary rigidity reflected here as in so much else the church from which it came: Thomas Hardy's *Under the Greenwood Tree* tells a moving story of how a 19th-century English vicar drove out the traditional fiddles from his country church and replaced them with an organ which he considered the only really proper instrument of ecclesiastical music. The same thing was happening in countless other places. Fiddles in England, drums in Africa. But both have come back today.

It was certainly the independent churches which gave the lead in the creation of a modern African Christian hymnology making use of the traditional patterns of African singing and a variety of instruments. In the last twelve years they have been followed with great vigour by the Catholic Church. In general it is the Protestant mission connected churches, wedded to the late 19th-century liturgy, that are here rather holding back. The immense enthusiasm with which, under the lead of men like Father Stephen Mbunga in Tanzania and Bishop Peter Dery in northern Ghana, the Catholic Church has transformed its church music is perhaps the single most encouraging thing that has happened in African Christianity in this decade. This is not yet true of all languages but it is true of a great many—Swahili, Bemba and Chewa, Igbo and Fon and many another. In some European countries the ousting of Latin from its central place in Catholic worship has been a musical disaster; in Africa it has been quite the opposite. The transformation of Catholic liturgy in the wake of the second Vatican Council has coincided with the cultural revival to produce a wave of musical creativity of the first importance. The restrained introduction of the drum into church worship, and of dancing too—as in the intensely beautiful and moving liturgy of Ndzon-Melen in the Cameroon—has all come together with the necessity of producing a new vernacular liturgy. Public worship remains the decisive centre of church life and the musical revolution is not significant simply in itself but for the effect it is having on the wider quality of Christian living. It has done much to remove the alienating dimension from those churches which have accepted its impact, but of course there are still many, both Protestant and Catholic, which have refused to budge one inch from the hymnbooks of seventy years ago.

For Catholics the cultural revolution in worship has not stopped with hymns. The new Zairean mass and the liturgy of Ndzon-Melen have gone further still in the Africanisation of ritual. While there is no question of altering the profound structure of Catholic liturgy, yet it is increasingly recognised that even the eucharistic prayers can be profitably re-expressed to reflect, indeed to grow out of, African life and culture. With several different eucharistic prayers already in use in the Church, there can be no reason to refuse others whose spiritual milieu is particularly that of Africa. One such, which has already been prayed in many African languages (though admittedly written by a missionary, Aylward Shorter) begins as follows:

> God, Father of our ancestors,
> friend in our midst,
> your children come before you.
> Here is your food!
> Here is your drink!
> These things are yours before they are ours.
> Now we are making a feast,
> but it is a thanksgiving;
> we are thanking God.

It is in the experience of vernacular prayer, both public and private, both formal and informal, and in the spirituality which grows up from such experience that the true roots for an authentic African Christianity will most surely be found. There has, however, in the last few years been less talk of African spirituality than of African theology. Can there be an African theology? Is there

49

one? If so, what are its characteristics? There is no doubt that Christian history has seen the development of almost innumerable theologies from the New Testament on. A Christian theology is a way of ordering, developing and discussing Christian revelation in the context of the world of the theologian. Christian revelation and Christian doctrine are not abstract systems; they can never be formulated nor fruitfully approached except in a context of time and place requiring a spelling out of intellectual and moral implications for society. Society changes both in its needs and in its capacity for penetrating the sense of the original biblical texts. Even within the same society different schools and different people draw out very different patterns of meaning and priority from the Bible, and they relate it in varying ways with the contemporary world. The sheer wealth of the Bible renders inevitable a vast pluralism within theological activity. In the past there have been Antiochene and Alexandrian theologies; western and eastern theologies; Thomist and Scotist theologies; Calvinist, Arminian; Evangelical, High Church, Liberal; German, English, and Greek theologies; so too without any measure of doubt there must be African theology. No, there must be many African theologies. The size of the Christian community in Africa, the variety of denominational experience, the immense variations between the human situation, the political and economic pressures—all this requires a pluralism of African theological experience and expression. Without it the churches would be maimed.

Where are we to look for African theology today? There can be no doubt that theology in the west has come to appear a rather academic business, carried on by university professors much as other academic disciplines. As the western model of university has been transplanted almost without change to Africa, so has this model of theology: there are now departments of theology and of religious studies in many African universities and out of these departments has come a significant beginning of academic African theology and academic theologians—scholars like Harry Sawyerr of Sierra Leone, Bolaji Idowu of Nigeria, John Mbiti of Kenya, Monsignor Tshibangu the Rector of the National University of Zaire. The departments over which these men have presided have naturally paid particular attention to the study and reappreciation of African traditional religions, for long so much neglected or despised in educated circles. The wheel has come full circle for they are now at the very centre of the academic stage.

The African theologian finds that the chief non-biblical

reality with which he must struggle is the non-Christian religious tradition of his own people, and African theology in its present stage is shaping as something of a dialogue between the African Christian scholar and the perennial religions and spiritualities of Africa. These religions were immensely rich and significantly varied—just as the kinship and marriage systems of Africa were highly varied. African tribes did not have uniform social, political and economic structures and as their religion was closely integrated with such structures, it would be a miracle indeed if all had had substantially the same religion. Of course their religions had common elements, but then so have all the religions of the world. It is immensely important that the theological dialogue with African traditional religion grows out of the richness of the latter and not out of some rather poor common denominator.

Europeans almost always underestimated the African sense of God in their earlier encounters, being much more struck by the strong consciousness of a wider spirit world—ancestors and natural forces—with its shrines and sacrifices. It may be that there were African peoples who had only a very slight sense of there being one God above all other spiritual beings or even none at all, as Okot p'Bitek claims of the Acholi; but the religions of most people included clearly enough both the one and the other. That is, however, true of people in many other parts of the world too. The balance between the two, on the other hand, greatly varied and it is precisely on that balance and the many ways that it could be conceived that the very real sense and finesse of a religion largely depends. For some people the reality of the one God may have been wholly dominant, anything else utterly subordinate; for others God was a remote being to whom one did not pray. A typology of African religions is not only of immense importance in itself; it can also serve to identify the range of Christian theologies and theological options. African Christian theology can grow out of African traditional religion both by empathy and by analysis.

'Take my face and give me yours' is the opening sentence of a moving Bushman prayer for immortality. It is in prayer and what can best be described as the spirituality of life that African traditional religion is best encountered in its rich and expansive diversity. It is not easy for a formal, written theology to draw upon such material without great impoverishment and even sheer misunderstanding which includes the imposition of categories drawn from quite other traditions. The Christian scholar, like many an academic in other fields, too easily finds in African traditional religion just that which he is looking for. While such a work as Mbiti's *African Religions and Philosophy* is proving an influential contribution to the literature of African theology, particularly as a work of initiation, there is a real danger here that African tradition be far too easily interpreted in a unitary way and precisely within the structures of western theological thought. In the development of theological concern there is also a danger that areas of traditional Christian doctrine which are not reflected in the African past disappear or are marginalised, and this includes almost anything specifically christological.

The religious authenticity which is being sought by current African theology is beyond all else an authenticity of continuity, first and foremost the continuity of God. Missionaries did indeed widely recognise the reality of this continuity by accepting an already existing vernacular African name for the God they themselves proclaimed instead of importing or inventing one, but they seldom made any attempt to build on this or interpret its fundamental significance. In recent years, however, the very considerable and beautiful body of proverbs and spiritual sayings in many languages which refer to God have been brought into some use in preaching and catechesis. What is now intended is to go far further in recognising that current African Christianity has in fact, and rightly, two primary sources of inherited wisdom and continuity: Christian revelation and tradition upon the one hand, African traditional religion upon the other.

'African theology' as it has been developing these last few years in teaching and writing, mostly in a rather academic and literary way and almost entirely through the medium of either English or French, by people almost all within the main mission-connected churches, has been throughout a theology of continuity. Monotheism, an enduring and filial relationship with one's ancestors, an ethic of community, these have been its most notable areas of concern. Discordant elements from the past have tended to be passed over. There is very little here about sin, about the failings of the past (on the African side), or again about Christ. A leading theologian can quote with approval the remark of an old person, a devout Christian, that when all is said and done the missionaries really brought nothing new in religion—they only brought a technology. The authenticity of African Christianity today is here found in a synthesis impatient with any setting up of barriers between the old and the new, or again between different Christian churches.

If African traditional religion is rather easily seen as having had an overall unity, African theology and the churches are entrusted with the task of reconstituting that unity today. There is here a striking contrast between theory and reality, so much so that Professor Mbiti, probably the best known Christian academic of eastern Africa, has hit out bitterly against what is actually happening today within the churches of his own country, particularly those standard bearers of authenticity, the independent churches: 'Christianity in Kenya has mushroomed denominationally, and the mushroom has now been turned into a messy soup. This excessive denominationalism is absolutely scandalous . . . this invites someone to call a halt; and if that someone is not the churches themselves; then it may well be the government. Christianity must not be allowed to become a cloak and cover for divisiveness in the country. . . .' He followed this up by calling on the government of Kenya to set up an 'effective, efficient and well-organised ministry of religious affairs'. One feels that the direction here is not wholly dissimilar from that of President Mobutu whose policy of religious authenticity has brought about the unification of the major Protestant churches in Zaire (other than the Kimbanguist) and the banning of most of the smaller independent churches.

And yet many would claim that it is just these churches which have most authentically Africanised Christianity and now constitute the true model of 'authenticity', so that there are both missionaries and many African Christians who argue that the mission-connected churches should strive to learn the message of these hitherto despised bodies. In other ways too the authenticity of the independent churches is in fact very different from that of 'African theology'. Despite the undoubted fact that they represent a profoundly African response to Christian faith, their spirituality *vis-à-vis* their own past is often one of discontinuity rather than continuity, at least at the specific level of religion. In regard to social custom they may frequently be more tolerant than the old missionaries, particularly in regard to polygamy (though the Kimbanguist Church takes a stronger anti-polygamy line than almost any mission church today), but in regard to religious practice most proclaim a total and indeed intolerant discontinuity and they do so precisely in the name of Christ. No missionary today would dare call for the burning of fetishes with the fervour and conviction of an African prophet. For the Aladura churches of Nigeria—surely one of the most vigorous groups of independent churches anywhere—traditionalists are pagans who need to be converted and that is that. There is no room for compromise here. As one of the leaders of the Celestial Church of Christ declared: 'They bow down to Idols while we bow down to God and to Jesus Christ.' One finds exactly the same thing among the Spirit churches of Rhodesia whose leaders from the outset not only publicly burnt traditional charms and medicines but mounted an all out attack upon every form of ancestor 'worship'. The destruction by Johane Maranke, leader of the African Apostolic Church, of the bull dedicated to his own family spirits was a symbolic act of great significance. It would seem wholly opposed to the sympathetic approach to ancestor cults advocated both by African theologians and liberal minded missionaries of the main churches.

If the university theologian sees in traditional religion the worship of the one God and identifies with it, the independent church leader in the village more often sees there instead a rival cult and a rival ministry offering salvation in a name other than Christ's. If the independent churches were not independent churches but missionary bodies, their position would be condemned as a most crass misunderstanding by the foreigner, and yet the independent churches are in general hailed—and particularly by the university theologians—as being the avant garde of African Christian authenticity! Clearly there are highly contradictory strands of authenticity here to be struggled with in the years ahead. The intolerance of the Spiritual Churches in regard to African traditional religion is not, nevertheless, an indication that they are themselves in some mysterious way foreign, but rather that the very depth of their Africanisation allows them no room to tolerate what they have replaced far more absolutely than the mission churches. Of course they have adopted a new 'foreign' principle—the absolute lordship of Christ—but they have then truly applied it in Africa. They have little of an explicit theology any more than has African traditional religion, but they have a praxis and a spirituality in which a theology is profoundly implicit. Their being is almost as an eruption of African traditional religion integrally transmogrified by faith in Christ: the human situation is the same, the solution is different.

This spirituality and praxis have taken to heart both the concerns and the techniques of tradition—the small community, the need for health here and now, the fears of sorcery and witchcraft, the proximity of spirits. Again all the material of religious culture is carried across, apparently almost unchanged—the type of melody, the hand-clapping, the ecstatic dancing, the appeal to visions, the interpretation of dreams. There is a continuity here which clearly the mission churches deliberately rejected and with which, in the concrete, most academic theologians of continuity feel ill at ease. But this very continuity in the religious tools serves and requires the discontinuity of message. Christ alone saves by the power of God, though he is served and manifested by countless angels. The spirits and the ancestors of tradition are uncompromisingly rejected at the level of religion, although their existence is by no means necessarily denied. The world is filled instead with the angels of God, it is to them that one must turn and Gabriel may well appear to the devout believer upon a Lagos beach.

Mu lidala lilahi
Mu lidala lilahi
Zingelosi bibixa zingubu zindabu
Mu lidala lilahi

In the good village
In the good village
The angels wear bright clothes
In the good village

So sang the members of many churches in a hymn very popular in Tiriki, Kenya, in the 1950s. The woman from whom it came declared that both words and tune were revealed to her in a dream.

Angels are not very popular today in the religious culture of the west, but they are immensely popular in Africa—and not only in the independent churches. While the religio-cultural revolution at the academic and middle class level reasserts the worth of ancestor veneration, that same revolution at village level does the opposite—it rejects the ancestors without compromise, replacing them within a domestic economy which calls for an awareness of spirits by a multitude of angels.

The praxis of Christian life in both the independent churches and many mission-connected churches too is one which takes dreams very seriously indeed: how many ministers have found their vocation through a dream vision! We must prepare ourselves during the day to dream well at night: to be open to God. Here as at so many other points it is impossible to say: this is African and not Christian. It is rather that a breakthrough of African tradition into Christian living is both validated and transformed by the discovery of biblical resonances and justification. The first few pages of the New Testament alone report some half dozen important dreams, yet the role of dreams was not part of the missionary message to Africa.

Fasting is another instance. Though an important element in Christian, and particularly Catholic, tradition, it has been steadily eroded in the modern practice of the mission churches, just as it has been strikingly embraced by many of the independent churches. For them the gospel saying 'There is no way of casting out such spirits as this except by prayer and fasting' is the very truth. They believe in the presence of the spirits, in the efficacity of the prayer and the fasting, and they practise as they believe. It sometimes appears as if representatives of the mission churches believe in none of the three, despite their theoretical emphasis on the importance of a biblically based Christianity. The discovery by the independents of their own model of African authenticity is at the same time a discovery of biblical authenticity as opposed to the demythologising liberalism fashionable in modern western churches.

It is especially during long fasts that the prophets of modern Africa see their major visions and experience their calls, much as did the prophets and leaders of the early Church, Paul and Barnabas included. Time and again fast and vision are linked together in the modern African experience even if—as in the case of Emanuel Opoku-pare, the Ghanaian founder of the Sacred Order of the Silent Brotherhood—the experience takes place in London, in the Kilburn Park Road, while studying on a Commonwealth Scholarship Award. 'I am the Light of the World. Rise up, break your fast and eat. . . . With your hands I shall heal, comfort and bless many.'

Across prayer and fasting, ecstasies and angels, a paraphernalia sometimes hardly distinguishable from that of non-Christian religion, what most of these churches are affirming without any final ambiguity is the power of God and of Christ (a single unbreakable concept) to save, to heal, to reassure, to provide comfort and consolation. There is a popular religion here, to be found alike in the independent churches, in the revival movements of the older Protestant churches and in some more deeply rooted sections of the Catholic Church, which is yet unmitigatedly Christ centred. When one has sat in a rural bus in Africa for several hours listening to a group of believers singing almost ceaselessly 'I am so glad that Jesus loves me' one will not doubt that. This common religion of Africa sits lightly enough on mission structures of any sort.

One of the greatest problems facing the cultural revolution is that of language. This may be illustrated by the recent history of Mozambique. Many people rightly condemned the Portuguese colonial government for its policy of 'Portugalisation'. All school teaching had to be in Portuguese and no attention whatsoever was paid to the many vernaculars. With political independence, it was hoped, this would surely be righted and the vernaculars would come into their own: there would be a cultural-linguistic independence too. In fact Frelimo has followed the exactly contrary course, stressing the teaching of Portuguese more than ever before. It sees the vernaculars as divisive and quite without the capacity to act as a media for a programme of rapid modernisation of a socialist kind. Almost all the independent governments of Africa have similarly stuck to a European language—English, French or Portuguese. Zambia would be quickly torn apart if Bemba became its official language and Nigeria might well face another civil war if Hausa, for instance, were to be chosen there. Only in Tanzania and Malawi has such a policy proved possible and, in the eyes of government, desirable—with Swahili and Chewa; though Kenya and Uganda have also theoretically opted for Swahili. It is by no means impossible to develop a language over a few decades into an adequate tool for modern education—Afrikaans and Welsh, Flemish and Hebrew are all examples of this. Swahili will most probably prove the same, even if a good many years will still be required. The immediate problem may be less a linguistic than a political one. In Tanzania it was a viable political option; in most African countries at national level it is at present not.

But is it intrinsically possible for an African cultural revolution to take place across a European tongue? Language is at the very heart of culture, African culture above all, though with the vast multiplicity of living languages it is at the heart of her problems as well. The rich growth of an African literature in English and French over the last fifteen years, the names of such men as Senghor, Soyinka, Achebe and Ngugi suggest that the answer to our question may be 'Yes'. And yet it remains a rather hesitant yes. The immense vigour of Africa's linguistic heritage, the determination of ordinary Africans to go on using their own languages, the very limited constituency that the European languages still possess on the continent (only a tiny proportion of the population is really fluent in any of them)—all this suggests that the cultural revolution is bound to go off at half cock until it takes the vernacular as seriously as Nyerere has taken it—not only insisting upon the steadily increasing use of Swahili throughout the country but himself contributing to the establishment of a vernacular literature both his own speeches and some distinguished dramatic translations—Shakespeare's *Juliasi Kaizari* and *Mabepari wa Venisi*.

If theology is not to be an élitist activity, essentially remote from the living roots of the churches, must it not too take the vernacular more seriously than it has done hitherto? The theology of Mbiti and Nyamiti, Idowu and Fasholé-Luke, Tshibangu and Agossou remains, despite its African concern, remarkably controlled in language and methodology by its European medium and by the European academic centres and traditions where its proponents studied and shone. The very different theology of the independent churches is essentially as vernacular as it is non-academic. Both are valuable strands within the cultural revolution and the Africanisation of Christianity, and both have their weaknesses. It may well be that a third locus of theological creativity is now developing—more pastoral and rooted in the local church and the rural community than that of the academics, more reflective and in touch with the world Church than that of the independent prophets. I am referring to the growing body of bishop-theologians, men like Sanon of Bobo-Dioulasso in Upper Volta, Sastre of Lokossa in Dahomey, Kalilombe of Lilongwe in Malawi.

None of these groups really conforms to President Mobutu's model of authenticity. Zaire has a larger Christian population than any other in independent Africa and its government's campaign for authenticity has now continued for several years. It is impossible not to take it with great seriousness. Citizen Engulu, State Commissioner of Political Affairs and Co-ordination of Party Activities, gave a major address on its meaning in Decembe 1974 which has become one of the basic documents for the course in Mobutism to be given in educational establishments: 'In our religion we have our own theologians. Our religion is based on belief in God the creator and the cult of ancestors. . . . In every religion and at all times there are prophets. Why should there no longer be any nowadays? God has sent us a great prophet, our wondrous guide Mobutu Sese Seko. This prophet is shaking us out of our torpor. He has delivered us from our mental alienation. He is teaching us how to love each other. This prophet is our liberator, our Messiah, the one who has come to make all things new in Zaire. Jesus is the prophet of the Hebrews. He is dead. Christ is no longer alive. He called himself God. Mobutu is not a god and he does not call himself God. He too will die but he is leading his people towards a better life. How can honour and veneration be refused to the one who has founded the new church of Zaire? Our church is the Popular Movement of the Revolution. Its head is Mobutu, whom we respect as the Pope is respected. Authenticity is our law.'

It may be that Mobutism will have no longer a life than Nkrumahism. Africa is prolific in movements and ideologies, prophets and authenticities. The cultural revolution has not a single form, and some of them will surely appear more transitory and less authentic than others—cloaks perhaps for new structures of alienation or for the establishment of a hard, unafrican, state absolutism. In the long run who will prove the more significant witness to African religious authenticity—Mobutu Sese Seko or Johane Maranke or John Mbiti or Peter Dery? They must pull in different ways, yet there can be no doubt that modern African society as a whole is deeply committed to the pursuit of authenticity—a cultural journey of discovery with its goal self-identity. And the church is utterly implicated in this pursuit. Its own soul is at stake. If some of the cultural nationalist forms advocated may be gravely destructive of Christian authenticity, this is not the first time, nor the first continent, in which that would have happened. There are forms of cultural nationalist authenticity essentially opposed to the catholicity of Christianity. Indeed the 'Christian nationalism' of Afrikaner South Africa already presents a warning of which black Africa could well take note. Yet there is also a national religious authenticity which is not only not opposed to an incarnational Christianity but is actually required by it. 'You may, and you must, have an African Christianity', Pope Paul told the African Catholic bishops at Kampala in 1969. It is, indeed, a perilous enterprise but in the vista of the Incarnation and the staggering numerical breakthrough of Christianity in this continent during the last hundred years, a supremely necessary one.

CHAPTER 4

Patterns of healing

One day in September 1975 in Herbert Macaulay Street, the very heart of Lagos, a middle-aged woman was dragged along the road, cursed, spat upon, and stoned to death. She had been accused of causing the death of many of her neighbours: 'You are a witch, you are a witch' the crowd cried.

Just fifty years before, on the other side of Africa, in what is today Zambia, there was one of the strangest and most terrible witch pursuits of modern times. A man named Tomo Nyirenda, a Watch Tower preacher, previously educated for six years at the famous Presbyterian mission of Livingstonia, took up the work of preaching and baptising among the Lala in central Zambia. Repent your sins and be baptised, was his message; in particular, repent your witchcraft. The Lala at the time were most desperately afraid of witches. There had never been so many of them, it seemed. The Anglican missionaries at Fiwila nearby described it as 'the worst place in the world for witchcraft', but there was little they could do about that. And then Nyirenda arrived, in April 1925. His simple gospel condemned witchcraft but encouraged kindness and hospitality and quickly brought about not only the mass baptism of entire villages but long services of hymn singing and prayer. A man of great spiritual forcefulness, the people at once identified him with 'the Son of God' *Mwana Lesa*. His preoccupation with the evil done by witches grew greater and greater; to call them to repent was clearly not enough. Far better to get rid of them once and for all. Tomo was soon claiming to identify witches when they were brought before him—much like an English 'witch pricker' of Stuart times—and once identified they were killed by drowning—a sort of extension of the mass baptisms. Those so identified hardly even struggled while the people as a whole were delighted: witchcraft is the source of terrible trouble and must be wiped out. People felt genuinely grateful to Tomo even though the witch had been one's sister or brother, or perhaps one's old mother. He was hailed as Prophet and Saviour and dozens of people were killed by him before he was arrested and tried by the colonial authorities.

Time after time witch eradication movements have swept across Africa, particularly Central Africa. They do not, of course, mostly result in the execution of the witches but in their detection and 'cure'. Frequently the identified witch has to swallow a medicine which, it is said, will bring about his death if ever he should return to his evil practices. Thirty years after Tomo Nyirenda another remarkable religious movement erupted in Zambia, this time among the Bemba—the Lumpa Church of Alice Lenshina, founded in 1955. It is quite probable that if Nyirenda had not been brought to killing his witches but only to exposing them or expelling them from the village community, then his movement too would have developed into an independent Christian church, relating certain stark but powerful elements of the Christian gospel to the immediate needs of the country people he was ministering to. Lenshina's message was only a little less simple than Nyirenda's and it had much the same content. It was expressed in beautiful Bemba hymns very different from the stiff translations of Victoriana used in the mission churches. Yet it too was to end in disaster when its millennialist claims clashed with those of triumphant nationalism to bring about the death of over seven hundred people in 1964 during fighting between Lenshina's followers and the newly elected government of Kenneth Kaunda. The Lumpa Church had grown out of a double tradition—upon the one side that of the independent church movement, upon the other that of the eradication of witchcraft and sorcery. It was a church of the elect called by Jesus Christ, firmly rejecting both beer and polygamy. Their faith and sense of vocation were expressed in Lenshina's many hymns, such as the following:

No slanderer, no troublemaker will enter the new Sion.
And you, my brother, you my sister, you will not enter either
Because you miss the Saviour Jesus Christ.

But the class of people which, above all others, will not enter Sion is undoubtedly that of witches and sorcerers:

You sorcerers, be on your guard,
You will face the Creator with the charms you prepare.

Or again:

Shout to the desert, shout
Leave beer and witchcraft.

The supreme attractions of Lenshina's Church were its claims to deliver people from the powers of sorcery and then the lasting hymn-singing fellowship it built up in its own segregated villages. The trouble with the deliverance from witchcraft is that it may not prove so lasting. A claim to eradicate witchcraft is almost always at least implicitly millennialist, that is to say it presupposes a moment of finality just about to arrive after which all these evil things will have disappeared for good. When no such moment arrives and, on the contrary, human sicknesses and sudden deaths continue to occur (the very things which until now could only be explained by the presence of witches or sorcerers), then either the whole eradication system is little by little discredited or some new malign influence, as yet untreated, is discovered and blamed. These must be the people who have refused to join the system. Thus Lenshina's followers at one moment strongly accused the local Bemba Catholic priest of being a sorcerer but proved unable to deal with him; on the contrary, he was a sturdy character and several of them found themselves in prison. In such circumstances the eradicated, cleansed area of society will either try to separate itself totally from the still polluted part or turn against it violently. In the case of the Lumpa Church both happened.

In contrast with attempts of this sort to grapple with the basic fears of African traditional society, most representatives of the mission-connected churches have, in a somewhat simple way, stuck to a straight denial that witchcraft has any reality at all, a denial which has brought with it more often than not an effective opting out from a whole crucial area of pastoral care. In some churches this, however, is now changing, and the change can be yet another example of the deep shift of emphasis which comes over a mission-connected church when the expatriate element finally recedes. One striking example of this is the Anglican Church of Tanzania where in 1974 and 1975 a catechist named Edmund John, the archbishop's brother, suddenly rose to prominence. From diocese to diocese and parish to parish he travelled round the churches holding a new, immensely popular form of 'healing mission', in which many sick people were treated but most especially were devils thrown out, witches identified and liberated. Before each such mission Edmund John walked round the church in the middle of the night with his Swahili Bible, reading the first nine verses of chapter 20 of Deuteronomy on preparation for war. During the main service hundreds of people who believed themselves to be possessed by spirits of one kind or another would be prayed over amidst a great noise of screaming and wailing until all were freed. For Edmund John the mission of healing was a battle with the devil for which he prepared himself by the most rigorous fasting. Such fierce asceticism soon helped to break down his constitution and he died in June 1975.

There is no doubt about the immense and enthusiastic response that village Christians in Tanzania gave to Edmund John. It could well be that in their church life they had been starved of something which they had been needing all along; it might also be that there are more fears of bewitchment, more experience of possession by spirits in the Tanzania of today than formerly. This could be a consequence of its ujamaa policy whereby people have been forced to leave their old homes and tiny hamlets to take up residence in much larger villages. In their old homes they had the graves of their ancestors close and, in consequence, friendly spirits to protect them. These they have lost. In the new unfamiliar communities they are at first more aware than ever of hostile spirits and of the sorcery of malevolent neighbours. In a similar situation in Zambia in 1971 much the same problem occurred. The government was trying to regroup people from rather isolated communities in Mambova, near Livingstone, but few were willing to avail themselves of the material advantages offered by the government at the new site. Their headman, Kamwi, put their point of view clearly enough: 'We want government services which we are being told about, but can't the Government do something about witchcraft which is worrying us ? We live in isolated villages to avoid mixing with these people who enjoy killing others and we want the Government to help us in any way before we can persuade our hearts to live together.'

It may well be such a situation which explains the vast welcome which Edmund John's ministry received just at a moment of village upheaval. But the sudden appearance of a Tomo Nyirenda, an Alice Lenshina, or an Edmund John is only the tip of a vast iceberg: the whole world of unexplained illness and misfortune, of spirit possession, of fears of bewitchment—things which are present all the time and yet have largely left the Christian churches baffled and unable to respond. Here, in matters of the most vital importance for millions of ordinary human beings, African concepts, biblical concepts, and modern western concepts of health and sickness both clash and intertwine.

No society can operate without both a theory of sickness and a practice of medicine, and African societies have certainly been no exception. Faced with illness of one sort and another, human beings need both something practical to do and a wider philosophy of explanation which renders ill health, bereavement and every form of misfortune somehow tolerable by establishing it within a wider frame of reference. By explaining things one at least partially copes with them, and one can be helped to cope by forces of social therapy and religious ritual which need not in any way affect the actual physical state of affairs but rather reconcile individuals and community to factors beyond their control.

African concepts of health and sickness were an absolutely integral part of the single mesh of social structure and religious consciousness inside which people lived unhesitatingly. They were inevitably challenged both in practice and in theory by the coming of Christian missionaries. It is a commonplace that in theory Africans regularly explained deaths (at least the deaths of any except the very old) and unexpected misfortune in terms of spiritual agencies. They did not deny that there is a natural causality of sickness, caused by the body simply breaking down or coming into contact with dangerous physical substances. A boil, a common cold, toothache, a regular stomach disorder did not require special explanation. More serious troubles too may be caused in some way by physical agencies and can be treated in a straightforward physical way. Bone setting, herbal medicines, bodily rest were accepted as normal physical treatment of physical disorders.

At the same time, for all the more unexpected and serious disorders, a second line of thought came into operation: why me and not him? Why this week and not last week? Why have two people in the same family been suddenly afflicted? To answer questions of this sort, a second type of causality was posited— one relating to spiritual forces. This duality of explanation, physical and spiritual, to be found in traditional African interpretations of sickness is not in fact so far different from a similar duality in the thinking of most Christians, but whereas the latter largely, though not wholly, relate the spiritual dimension to God alone, Africans on the contrary seldom related it to God but rather to the activities of their ancestors, other spirits or—alternatively— malevolent neighbours (who may, of course, have set the spirits on). The deep African sense of the morality of the universe and all that happens therein required that a 'moral' explanation be given for sudden or undeserved misfortune. They were, one may say, too committed to the primacy of order to accept an explanation of the random in matters of importance. It was, as a consequence, necessary for good treatment to tackle both the physical ailment and the deeper moral 'ground' for the trouble. In roughly ascending order of danger: one's ancestors might be displeased with one for some just cause and need to be placated and their forgiveness obtained; some other more hostile spirit may have invaded one's life and needs to be thrust out or persuaded to leave one alone; some neighbours may have cast a spell in return for a real or imagined slight; a witch may have eaten your child's inside and so have caused its death.

The answer in every case is to call in a spiritual expert of one sort or another and see what he or she can do to help. She may be a spirit medium who can interrogate the spirits who are causing the trouble; he may be a clan priest who can prescribe certain sacrifices to the ancestors; he may be a professional in detecting the influence of a local witch. Whatever it is, there will first be a discussion in which the hopes and fears of those involved are revealed, the unsettled quarrels with neighbours, half-submerged feelings of guilt in regard to 'pietas' (a dead ancestor may be punishing one for disregarding the wishes of one's living parents), fears of some old woman half ostracised by the neighbourhood whose mumbled imprecations are only too well passed on and commented upon.

The total treatment—discussion, ritual, the application of various potions, the trance of a medium, the atmosphere of high tension and expectation preliminary to the interrogation or ejection of a spirit—all this forms a pattern of individual and group therapy out of which may well come the reconciling of individual conflicts, the clarification of role, the release of feelings of guilt, together with a needed sense of confidence in facing up to one's actual physical troubles. While none of this may greatly help in the curing of certain ailments, it will be of very great use for many others—both mental illnesses of varying degrees of seriousness and that large area of sickness now recognised even in the west as truly psychosomatic: migraine, ulcers, certain types of paralysis, various bodily aches. Even for germ produced diseases which may kill or may not, the difference between the two results may depend upon the moral resistance of the patient which can be greatly fortified by traditional treatment.

While the effectiveness of a fair amount of this treatment should not then be questioned, it remains linked, even necessarily embedded in, a world view: the religion of the society in which the various activities of ancestors, of spirits, of sorcerers and witches are all an integral part. It was consequently inevitable that the medical systems, just as the marriage systems, of Africa be challenged by missionaries proclaiming a different religion containing within it what they saw as a very different interpretation of sickness and its causes. The inevitability of conflict was, unfortunately, compounded by ignorance. Missionaries generally failed to distinguish the doctor from the disease and easily identified the intentionally beneficial activities of local practitioners endeavouring to protect their clients from evil with the evils they were fighting. He became a 'witch-doctor', as evil as a witch, when in fact he saw himself as opposed to witches and all they stand for. This was not made easier by the admitted fact that there were and are people claiming to be able to handle both 'white' medicine and 'black'—both helpful and harmful. But there was a wide range of African medical practitioner from the bone-setter to the medium at the shrine of a spirit or long dead hero, whose functions and sense of self-identity were vastly different.

The most perplexing area of all is probably that of spirit possession, a phenomenon as varied and common today as in the past. It may be a private sickness—either the passing experience of a young girl or a state of psychological disequilibrium continuing for years; it may equally be the tool of an individual healer or an institution of public order. The spirit medium of a major shrine may be as respectable, as traditionalist, and even as predictable in his trances as the spiritual leaders of any other well established religious body. But the spirit medium of a new cult-shrine may have very different things to say and will be appealing, of course, to different sources of authority: he may even claim today to be the spokesman of the spirit of the Virgin Mary or the Apostle Matthew, if living in an area now heavily christianised. When, in the 1890s, Owamekaso, head among the spirits of the Calabar heroes and a major authority in Kalabari religion, called for the execution of all Christians because they were 'spoiling the town', another well known if more peripheral and independent spirit was telling people in the same town that they should all become Christians since the old days were nearly over.

Spirit possession, while not without its dangers, is something of a recognised language through which both communal and individual problems can be uncovered and talked out with a frankness not possible in common talk. Its primarily beneficial character does need to be contrasted with that of witchcraft and its eradication, to which a prudent Christian attitude is likely to be very different.

There are societies in Africa for which 'witchcraft' and the larger concept of 'sorcery' are not clearly distinguishable, but it seems to be widely true that there is an idea of witchcraft prevalent remarkably similar to the popular notions of it current in the past throughout Europe and, perhaps, in some form in every pre-scientific society. It is society's worst collective nightmare, a final explanation of undeserved misfortune, far more irrational—if one may so describe it—than belief in the casting of spells or the inter-vention of ancestors. Belief in witchcraft is in the activities of people—predominantly women, and even elderly women, though not always—who ride on wild animals or fly through the air at night, dance on graves, eat the bodies of their victims, have familiars (companion animals of one sort or another) and in general cause death or disaster without apparently ever going near the people they are affecting or having any normal reason for doing so. People can believe in witchcraft without ever identifying a witch or being too worried about their presence and anti-witchcraft dances may often not be intended as more than a generalised, though profoundly serious, assertion about evil, its moral sources and physical effects. A witch specialist is someone who intends to free society of a terrible evil, and even if this does involve the killing of recognised witches, this is seen more as a cleansing of the community than as the punishment of criminals (it is widely admitted that witches may even be unaware of the terrible things they have done).

Sorcery on the other hand, can be described as the conscious deliberate act of harming others by the use of special charms and the invocation of spirits. It is a recognisable form of behaviour which undeniably to some extent exists at the sociological level, as witchcraft does not. While at one time anthropologists liked to contrast these two very sharply, today they recognise that in practice in very many societies there is no such precise distinction: the idea of the one merges into that of the other, and while a supposed witch may be believed to ride on a hyena she is more likely to be accused first of putting a spell upon a relative who failed to help her repair her roof or a junior wife who displaced her in her husband's affections. 'Witchcraft' and 'sorcery' are opposite poles of interpretation for a single extended range of fear and otherwise inexplicable experience, rather than names for two quite separated 'things'.

It is difficult, indeed impossible, to know how far witch beliefs in the past in Africa produced the execution of supposed witches. Most anthropological and sociological studies of the subject were made in the benign Indian summer of colonialism when people had generally accepted that the administration would not tolerate such things. Hence an anthropologist's description may give a very much more anaemic impression than the unbridled internal dynamic of a system would really have warranted. Certainly in some times and places witches were regularly killed, as during the famous annual witchcraft trials at Lake Eni in Nigeria to which accused witches were brought from far afield. Whether such activities were ever such as to rival in scale the terrifying witch hunts of 16th- and 17th-century Europe one may doubt, remembering for instance how sixty-three women were burnt in one year alone, 1562, in the small German town of Wiesensteig. But, of course, both in Europe and in Africa it is of the nature of witchcraft beliefs that they long lie semidormant, suddenly flare up in a wave of ever wilder accusations, and then almost equally quickly die away as the accusers themselves grow discredited. A real witch hunt is never part of the social system; it is what happens when one rather mysterious element in a society's sanctions runs amok.

In a fairly balanced African society these things may be used with only a rare individual coming too greatly to grief. Those in authority may accuse young subversives; the young may accuse old dodderers (or their wives) who keep too tight a grip on power; in situations of unstructured personal conflict almost anyone may come under suspicion—perhaps not unlike accusations of inefficiency in a western institution suffering from strain under the winds of inflation. The more society as a whole is suffering from pressure and a sense of malfunctioning is prevalent, the more personal accusations multiply and the more likely is it that some among them will be followed up with decisive seriousness. Witchcraft accusations remain to some extent in a class apart because in regard to them no rational evidence can really be offered—they can only be established or rejected across some form of mystical 'ordeal'—while the terrible character of what is implied in them can so easily trigger off an equally terrible revenge.

At the end of it all the witchcraft accusation represents the deepest and most universal expression of man's irrational fear of man, his tendency in a world of pain and tragedy not to create a community of compassion but to take out his agony on a fellow creature.

19th- and 20th-century western Christianity long tended

either to put all this down rather indiscriminately to the working of the devil, or to ignore it all in perplexity as a curiosity of African life which would go away the quicker the less was said about it. Within the mission environment African medicine was to be replaced wholesale by western medicine. For the most part Africans were willing enough to accept the latter, once they had seen that in fair part it actually worked—it was welcomed as an extension to, or improvement upon, their own physical medicine. There has seldom been any marked or prolonged reluctance to make use of missionary hospitals. On the contrary, people walk very far to attend them, often finding them an improvement upon those of government. This is certainly not one in technique, for they are in general far poorer than their government counterparts; it is rather that they have shared something of the double approach to sickness—the recognition that the spirit must be treated at the same time as the flesh. The old mission hospital had its chapel in the centre, its public prayers as well as its medicines; it frequently had no qualified doctor but was directed by a sister or brother whose length of experience and charismatic personality drew patients from all parts. It was a curious thing in the 1960s to see mission hospitals deliberately break down this dual African character under pressure, maybe, of a western funding body which insisted upon 'higher' standards, a more impersonal and clinical approach. The charismatic sister was replaced by a string of qualified doctors with no knowledge of the language and recruited on short term contracts.

At the same time the missionary hospitals even at their best could not respond to all the medical needs of African man and the traditional systems survived and even thrived in new forms though their clients, if Christian, might well find themselves liable to excommunication from their own churches. They survived because, of course, western hospitals were anyway too few and far between to offer a very effective alternative: your native practitioner is in the village, your nearest western dispensary twenty miles away; but they also survived because to some considerable extent they worked (and no system of medicine is anyway more than partially effective); they survived most of all because they were crucial parts of a total socio-cultural system which continued to be the framework of life and thought for the large majority of people.

Increasingly, with the growth in size of the Christian community, this side of traditional culture as every other side passed into that community and pressed for some sort of structural recognition which the mission churches had largely failed to provide. Probably here, more than in any other segment of life, is to be found the chief source of strength and key to self-identity of the main stream of the independent churches. An apparent overstress by missionaries on a scientific, nonspiritual approach to healing, coupled with the manifest failure of western medicine to protect people from such dangers as the influenza epidemic of 1918 triggered off in some quarters a complete rejection of medicine in favour of faith-healing. One such movement, which had already begun some years earlier, was that of the Bamalaki in Uganda. For them western medicine was but another form of African medicine—reliance on things. Faith in God called one to rely on him alone. Here as elsewhere African Christians found inspiration in the Bible for ways of behaviour other than those commended by missionaries. The New Testament had nothing to say about scientific medicine, but it had much to say about the casting out of devils, faith healing through prayer, spiritual gifts much akin to the trances and achievements of the traditional medium. All across Africa independent churches, while divided on whether or not to reject all use of western medicine, have adopted services of prayer healing dependent upon the throwing out of spirits, the ecstatic utterance of strange tongues, but also the acceptance of long hours of intense prayer of a fairly conventional kind, all based upon a deep sense of the relationship of physical health to spiritual health and the will of God. For many churches sickness is the prime initiating point of religious life, and their concern for it in an idiom which is local and traditional their main attraction.

Let us look for a moment at Zion City, the church headquarters of Bishop Mutendi in Rhodesia. It is in fact a hospital. In the centre of it is his own home and huts for his fourteen wives and fifty children. Nearby is the church and other ecclesiastical buildings with, just beyond them, the two hundred huts of the hospital. When someone arrives at Moriah, he is sprinkled with holy water to cleanse him of all that is impure and expel any evil spirit. Then the full time clerk notes down the patient's particulars, while the patient is given a piece of paper containing the name of the prophet who will later diagnose his illness. The 'boarding-master' makes sure that one of the huts is prepared for the newcomer. The hospital register speaks of pain in chest and stomach, barrenness, the presence of evil spirits, a general sense of being bewitched. In the following days the common prayer and work, the atmosphere of community, the sprinklings with holy water, interviews with lesser prophets and then one with Mutendi himself and the much appreciated laying on of hands—all this may contribute to the patient both feeling better and deciding to become a permanent member of the Zionist Christian Church.

'This place is like Bethsaida' declared Evangelist Mordechai during a sermon at Moriah in 1965. 'Just as the power in olden days had come through great personages such as Abraham and Jacob, it now derives from the God of Mutendi and Enginasi Lekhanyane. Mutendi's power is stored away like the grain of a farmer's co-operation. He can cure you of all ailments. Assuredly he is the man of God!'

There are prophets and healing churches by the score in Ghana and Nigeria, Kenya and South Africa of whom quite the same is claimed. But differences in both theology and method can, nevertheless, be marked. Some employ an exuberant, ecstatic, even violent therapy with much shouting, trance-like behaviour and repeated laying on of hands; others have developed the calmer approach one senses in Bishop Mutendi's hospital while still concentrating upon the healing of specific physical complaints; others again—and one thinks of Joseph Diangienda in Zaire or Johannes Galilee Shembe in Natal—now appear to give priority to a wider therapy of carefully listening to complaints and counselling, very different from the more intense charismatic healing of sickness carried on by their fathers, Simon Kimbangu and Isaiah Shembe. While there are many small spirit churches which, particularly at the outset, appear to be little more than clinics for spiritual healing, the tendency is for the area of their concern to grow steadily in relation to the stability of their membership. In a church of the second generation healing may well cease to keep its originally dominant position although the special rituals of the healing service with its evocative recalling of the church's early days remains important. Here as in the field of education there seems to be something of a secret law impelling each body in the direction of the old established churches. If every church begins with the miracles of St Mark's gospel, every church ends its second generation with the preoccupations of the pastoral epistles to Timothy and Titus. The inner mechanism of New Testament development is a remarkable key to the evolution of a new church.

When Josiah Oshitelu first felt a religious vocation in Nigeria

in the 1920s it was less to be a healer than a receiver and pro-
claimer of revelations, and yet the body he founded, the Church
of the Lord (Aladura), was very much a church of healing, a
church indeed in which all medicine was rejected. 'It is forbidden',
declared the 1938 Constitution, 'to go to doctors or to use medicine
of any kind . . . we trust in heavenly healing in this church . . . the
power of herbs has been ended, the power of medicine reduced to
vanity, the power of incantation exterminated.' But as other sides
of the church's life grew in the estimation of members, so did
this need to reject secular medicine diminish. In 1962 Oshitelu was
able to say that 'We have no absolute law against going to doctors
and hospitals.' There can be no doubt that church members are
doing so increasingly. In this matter the Aladura movement is
divided for while the Christ Apostolic Church completely rejects
the use of medicine, Cherubim and Seraphim accept it; the
Church of the Lord appears to be moving from one position to the
other while, of course, maintaining its important five hour monthly
services for healing.

The attitude of the Church of the Lord (Aladura) to health
and sickness does not now appear so far different from that of
some mission-connected churches who have rediscovered the
ministry of spiritual healing and practise it themselves. Doubtless
in this they have been influenced by movements such as Aladura;
they have also been affected by a revival of faith healing, pente-
costal prayer and exorcism now spreading all across North America
and Europe. But it is clear how deep is the continuity of approach
between the healing of traditional Africa and that embraced by
independent Christian churches. How far is this to go? What one
detects in many churches here as elsewhere is a continuity with
the past in the concerns they respond to and the complex of ritual
and social therapy they employ rather than in any final religious
interpretation. They do not for a moment deny the presence of
spirits to be cast out, witchcraft spells to be loosed, but faced
with them they assert the power of God to free and to restore. In
practice there seems to be a wide range of response, at one end
clearly controlled by a Christian sense of God and Christ; at the
other it is still rather deeply embedded in the religious metaphysic
underlying traditional treatment.

Problems multiply at both the pastoral and the theological
level. Some prophets only too clearly continue in Christian dress
the customary role of the witchfinder and are widely accepted in
this role by Christian and non-Christian alike. There are parts of

Rhodesia where people who think themselves bewitched or their child killed by a witch are today as likely to go to a Zionist prophet as to a traditional *nganga*. While the approach of the prophet varies there are many whose reaction is to 'discover' the witch responsible—probably someone thought to be harbouring illwill towards the sufferer—and while this may bring about forgiveness and reconciliation, its consequence is frequently ostracism, physical assault or even suicide.

The following account, given in court by a woman whom a prophet named Kiwanyana had identified as a witch, is only one among many. She was identified during a prophetic service. The following day was Sunday: 'Next morning on Sunday, my husband, my daughter and I were sitting in our kitchen when I heard a party of Zionists arrive in our yard. They were singing and throwing ash on the hut roofs and into the huts. They entered the hut. I was sitting in the middle of the hut and they danced around me. There was a fire in the fireplace—they removed the burning coals leaving the glowing embers. Accused (Kiwanyana) then arrived, he danced round and round, then he climbed on top of my shoulders. He then took me by the ears and threw me to the ground. He then caught me by the throat and choked me. Accused then picked me up and put me in the fireplace. He put grass around me and when this grass did not ignite he lit it with a match. He repeatedly asked me if I *loya'd* (bewitched). Accused held me in the fire. I tried to break away but he forced me back. He kept saying that I was a witch. After I had been badly burnt I admitted being a witch but I am not a witch.'

While the prophets are seeking in principle to cure not to punish, the cure presupposes confession and confession can hardly be obtained without force and fear. One sees only too clearly here the process whereby popular witchcraft beliefs are given an added and still more deadly cutting edge within a Christian context.

There is, however, a theological attempt to vindicate in this field too the moral propriety of African tradition by asserting an objective validity in the concept of witchcraft. So Professor Idowu, for example, asserts that 'Witches exist in Africa. This is the basis of the strong and deeply rooted belief in witchcraft.' Again Dr Erivwo has urged that 'Christians ought to recognise that there is witchcraft, that it is both a subjective and objective reality emanating from the Devil'. Clearly a great many issues are involved here and there are schools of Christian thought in other continents which would undoubtedly support these theologians. Moreover no sociologist would deny that 'sorcerers' do in some sense exist—there exist people who believe themselves to be such and are so accepted by their neighbours—and in many vernacular languages there is no absolute linguistic distinction between the sorcerer and the witch. Hence it is not so easy to disagree absolutely with Professor Idowu. The Bible gives strong support to belief in the Devil and this cannot easily be rejected on specifically Christian grounds. Nevertheless if the New Testament has much to say about diabolical possession, it gives little countenance to a belief in witchcraft in the stricter and generally accepted sense. Both history and sociology suggest that while fears of being bewitched make only too much sense in a world of uncertainty, sudden disaster and village tensions, the really demoniac phenomenon is witchcraft accusations and their snowballing and not the causality of the misfortunes they feed upon.

Certainly the horrendous history of European witch-hunting from the 15th to the 17th century, so much encouraged by ecclesiastical and theological sanctioning of age-old peasant beliefs which had found no Church recognition in earlier periods, should offer a warning to the African Christian church of today. The recognition of spirit possession is one thing: as such it is clearly a fact and one requiring pastoral care. Its recognition does not carry with it any imputation of moral responsibility. The matter of witchcraft is another. Once one admits its reality one cannot avoid making accusations and over the most serious matters. The moral horizon is a quite different one. Witchcraft accusations may grow in intensity at a time of social dislocation; if they are somehow countenanced by the proponents of Christian truth they may take on a wild new certainty of a very simplistic kind, while the concept of witchcraft is so evil that once its existence is admitted there can seem a terrible logic in a campaign for its eradication, ruthless as that may have to be. Is it not here above all that a Christian view of sickness and death does clash quite decisively with the philosophy of African tradition? Spirit cults and witchcraft beliefs imply both a refusal to accept that misfortune is not morally imputable (and, of course, many Christians—Puritans above all—have also found that hard to accept) and a dependence upon lesser spiritual causalities because there is no adequate recognition that the great power of the one God could really be concerned with this or that side of one's own small life.

The High God of African tradition, the God of the Bible, the Christian God, does not have mediums; he does not as a matter of fact 'possess' people in this way. And yet his voice is heard. The Christian gospel would not be itself if it did not essentially assert the irrelevance of 'possession' and the non-existence of witchcraft. The very real experience of the one and the agonising fear of the other have to be overcome neither by the more powerful possession of a greater medium, nor by accusations against one's neighbours and a campaign of eradication, but by the confident sustained assertion of the power and loving mercy of God in Christ. That assertion too can be a social fact. Moreover the Christian gospel can never accept the non-attribution of the world and what is in it to God. Just as food is to be blessed in recognition and eaten with gratitude, so are the herbal remedies of Africa and the more sophisticated medicines of Europe to be accepted and made use of with a finally religious motivation. By and large Christian churches in Africa refuse to abandon secular medicine and they are right so to do, both in terms of straight-forward human need and of the implications of the revelational claims they make. As a matter of fact church hospitals are quite as much appreciated in the Africa of today as they ever were, parti-cularly in the more remote rural areas, and Church authorities would be very unwise to question their value both as a means of practical service and as a proper expression of the gospel. If conducted with sensitivity and a spirit of prayer, they can very much play their part in the wider struggle with fear and unexpected misfortune. The nursing nun or the devoted African medical assistant at a remote dispensary can be kept just as busy as the most successful prophet of healing. All three finally intend to give expression across a pattern of human care to the power and mercy of God.

There is another little church in Rhodesia, stemming from rather a different ecclesiastical tradition. That of St Francis near Rusape was founded by Francis Nyabadza, a breakaway from the Anglican diocese. While normally using the Anglican hymnal to which they were accustomed, they have composed one extra hymn of their own. It was written to remind them of a sermon preached by their present leader, Basil Nyabadza, when asked by neighbours to pray at the site of a new home so as to drive away evil spirits. It is very often sung.

Ari Mambo we wamambo,
  Tenzi we watenzi,
Jesu Kuwamba me kuguma,
Apana anoyenzana naye.
Wakagara ku gwenga,
Apana anoyenzana naye.

He is King of Kings,
  Lord of lords,
Jesus, the beginning and the end,
There is no other like him.
He lived in the wilderness,
There is no other like him.

In these simple lines the spirits are neither affirmed nor denied as an objective reality. Faced with the fears and failures of man, the absolute power of God manifested in Jesus is recognised, welcomed as unique and accepted as sufficient.

CHAPTER 5

Power, politics and poverty

In July 1969 Pope Paul VI arrived at Entebbe, Uganda, for the first papal visit to Africa. Scores of thousands of ordinary people had assembled to welcome him, coming from many countries, but there were also five heads of state present to do honour to the Bishop of Rome. Beside Milton Obote, President of Uganda, stood Julius Nyerere of Tanzania, Kenneth Kaunda of Zambia, Michel Micombero of Burundi and Grégoire Kayibanda of Rwanda. Their gesture in coming to Uganda on this occasion a decade after independence illustrates something of the relationship which has emerged between political leadership and church leadership in many parts of the new Africa. Fifteen years earlier Nyerere had been a teacher in a Catholic mission school, now he was one of the chief wielders of power in Africa—both direct political power in one important country and the wider power of being the continent's leading political guru.

Kaunda too had been a teacher as his father was before him. There can be no doubt that in the Zambia of the 1920s his father, David—a simple mission teacher, preacher and finally ordained minister—was really one of the most powerful, the most influential of people: a man who by the tenor of his life inspired the imagination of his fellows and pointed a whole society towards its future. By 1969 his son wielded a power, partly similar, partly of quite another kind though he wielded it, from the splendour of State House, Lusaka. He has himself meditated upon the difference, recognising his study at State House to be 'a far cry indeed from the old mission house at Lubwa'. 'This is indeed a grand setting for the son of a poor preacher. Around me are symbols of that most desired and yet dangerous of all commodities—power. And this is as good a point as any from which to start, with power, for that is what most of my life has been taken up with; how to get it, how to control it, how to share it.'

There is plenty of power to be got and to be controlled in the many states of today's Africa. The great question is: what is it used for? And how do the churches relate to it? But one thing which remains true is that most people in Africa have very little power. The coming of political independence did not bring in most countries any effective transfer of power into the hands of the masses, but into those of a small élite. The masses remain exceedingly poor, mostly illiterate, probably even more remote from the mechanisms of even local power than in colonial or precolonial times. Every country has its rich élite—perhaps 1% in Upper Volta, 5% in Kenya, 20% (almost all white) in South Africa. But Africa as a whole is a continent of poverty—the United States has a *per capita* income about fifty-five times, and the United Kingdom one about twenty-five times, that of many African countries. The common people are gripped by their poverty across the whole shape of their lives. It is admittedly a poverty which they take for granted and one which may well be less humiliating and far less humanly destructive than many other poverties in the world: because it is in most parts of Africa a poverty of the self-employed and a poverty which coheres with the rich cultural inheritance of a structurally viable community. African poverty is, originally, the expression of a limited traditional technology and a hard climatic environment. It has first to be interpreted in terms of the economic level and material achievement of its own society and not in those of another, exploiting, society. This primary poverty is, however, increasingly affected by external forces or is even quite subsumed within a new type of poverty of exploitation manifest in many parts of the continent but above all in South Africa, both rural and urban. Here African poverty (often materially worse than that of seventy years ago) is the reverse of white affluence. It is no more the poverty of people within a poor society but the poverty of people within a rich society, which is quite a different thing. Elsewhere too poverty is increasingly the consequence of the operation of external influences; it is more and more dependent upon the wider world. Its existence and toleration then become a moral outrage when compared with what the affluent world, which has made so much out of some parts of Africa, takes for granted.

A few rich and many very poor people—that is the common shape of Africa, white ruled or black ruled. The stark contrast presents the main underlying thread of moral concern. It is not then surprising that when Nyerere came on a state visit to Britain in November 1975 he chose poverty to be the theme of what was probably his most important public address. He began it by declaring that 'It would be almost absurd for me not to talk about this subject' and, faced with it, he called for 'an act of political will'. Power at grips with poverty—is that the true picture of political Africa in the 1970s?

To answer that question one must first cast a wide glance over the continent today. Nyerere is, after all, by no means a typical African ruler and the continent-wide picture of contemporary government is a very different one from that presented by Tanzania. It is a picture with great economic and political complexity. On the one hand are islands of great prosperity and the sort of power which goes with prosperity—white South Africa, white Rhodesia, the copperbelt, Abidjan, Nairobi, the booming oil economy of coastal Nigeria, though each is closely surrounded by an urban proletariat at least as poor as its rural counterpart. Every African country has something of such an island—be it little wider than an international hotel, the air-conditioned home of the president, a miniature university campus. But beyond the island are the rural masses, a minority of whom are fairly prosperous farmers of cotton, cocoa or coffee, but most of whom are hardly more than subsistence cultivators and many of whom are decidedly worse off than they were fifteen years ago. There are now more mouths to feed while world prices for most primary materials have steadily deteriorated in real terms. Beyond these are the inhabitants of large areas where the system has almost broken down completely leaving famine and civil war, and sometimes both at once. Over the last decade there have been long periods when considerable areas of the continent—in the southern Sudan, northern Ethiopia, eastern Zaire, Chad, eastern Nigeria, northern Mozambique and eastern Angola—have had next to no government at all.

From one point of view Africa today is divided between civilian governments and military governments. Despite all the army coups there remains a remarkable number of civilian rulers who have been in power for many years. Not only Vorster and Smith, but Senghor and Houphouet, Kenyatta and Banda, Nyerere and Kaunda. All in all they remain Africa's most respected rulers, but they have been joined by a larger number of military men, the victors of one or another coup. Some of these, like Colonel Acheampong of Ghana, remain clearly professional soldiers generally justifying their presence in government on grounds of a temporary necessity; others, such as Mobutu or

Eyadema of Togo become after some years essentially civilian heads of state, basing their rule on a one party system and an ideology which merges each in its own way elements of nationalism, cultural revival or authenticity, and socialism. In this they hardly differ from the civilians. The significant divide is not, then, a military/civilian one which straddles the more important groups. Both military and civilian rulers are to be found today upon the left wing and upon the right, and it is noticeable that the ending of Portuguese empire in southern Africa has brought to power liberation movements led by both: Samora Machel is a soldier, Agostinho Neto a civilian.

Neither can there be a classification based upon the practice of western democracy—governments which adhere to it and those which don't, if only because there is really no country in Africa which retains its generally recognised essentials.

Such unanimity may be a sound indication that at present it is simply not workable, although it remains the ideal for many Africans and one may wonder whether Ghana's second democratic attempt under Dr Busia might not have worked if the army had not ended it with the thinnest of justifications. But it is clear that a western type of democratic system is effectively rooted in too small a section of society to withstand such pressures. Some countries, to wit South Africa and Rhodesia, have retained all the trappings of liberal democracy and a multi-party system, but have by law excluded more than 80% of the population from taking any proper part in it. Others have abolished any pretence of parliamentary government. In practice each country is controlled through a single dominant party which may or may not make use of parliamentary forms, while alternative parties have either been banned by law or rendered ineffectual. If South Africa and Rhodesia retain the elements of a western multi-party system, it is still true that the Nationalists in the one (after more than twenty-five years unbroken rule) and the Rhodesia Front in the other occupy a position not dissimilar to that of UNIP in Zambia or the MPR in Zaire. And each is very strongly tied to the policy and personality of its leader. The most genuinely democratic systems remain those, such as that of Tanzania, which combine the framework of a single party with manhood suffrage, regular elections and a choice of candidates in each constituency. In Tanzania at least cabinet ministers are still in danger of losing their seats in a general election.

This points towards what may be the most significant

division between African governments—those which retain and those which do not retain a serious concern for the wishes and the interests of the mass of the population. Leadership comes from the élite, whether it be military or civilian, left wing or right wing (though General Amin at one extreme and Samora Machel at the other are in some ways exceptions to this), but only very few retain any effective bridge linking their rule to the consent of the masses and relating their policies to the needs of the many, not the few. The plight of Africa is indeed such that, even with good intentions—and most new governments start out with good intentions—it can be extremely difficult to manage either of these things, and the overall picture remains one of a growing divorce between the privileged and the government upon the one hand, and the vast majority of people upon the other. While the racial discrimination between minority and majority in South Africa and Rhodesia greatly hardens the division by legislation and embitters the majority (particularly, of course, because it forces into the excluded majority individuals who on account of wealth, education and profession would elsewhere be natural members of the minority), their fundamental pattern is comparable.

This striking inequality between an affluent élite linked to the wealthy of the wider world, whose local representatives they inevitably are, and a struggling proletariat, rural and urban is—of course—good ground for revolution of every sort and the spread of Marxism in particular. The situation is still too new and too fluid in black ruled Africa for major movements of class unrest to have occurred, but there are already some seven Marxist or near Marxist governments in Africa and the appeal of Marxism is almost sure to grow. Whether the Marxism of a government necessarily enables it to break away from the wider pattern of governmental élitism is another matter. Whether, for instance, the daily proclaimed Marxism of President Kerekou of Dahomey (now Benin) makes his policy appreciably different from that of his 'right-wing' neighbour President Eyadema of Togo, only time will tell.

But the ending of the Portuguese colonial empire has certainly brought with it a major new element of radicalisation in African politics. The talk in Mozambique today is not of 'African Socialism' but of 'Scientific Socialism'. Frelimo and MPLA stand in a different ideological tradition and have come to power in a sharply different way from the governments of French or English speaking Africa—though Sekou Toure is clearly something of a forerunner here. Their position is critical alike of the west, of the churches and of African tradition. If they urge a cultural revolution it will not be so as to resurrect the values of the precolonial past but rather to sweep them away: a new Marxist government may be as intolerantly antipolygamist as a new evangelical church.

How profound an effect the coming to power of Frelimo and MPLA will have upon the wider politics of black Africa, it is too early to say, but during its first year of power Frelimo has followed a line not so dissimilar to that of its neighbour TANU in Tanzania. These two movements do represent in concrete terms a very deliberate radical alternative to the politics of élitism and inequality so manifestly dominant in many other parts of the continent, both white ruled and black ruled. Whether they are successful in carrying their policies through, and whether the consequences prove markedly beneficial for the poor are different questions. The sheer poverty of both countries, the controlling power of a wider world economy from which they cannot break loose, internal failure to translate fine theory into sound practice, the thrall of village tyrants now newly decked out as local party commissars—all this and much else may combine to undermine the success even of a Nyerere or a Machel.

Where do the churches stand within the politics of modern Africa? What power do they have to influence the course of events and how do they use it?

The political role of the churches in Africa is an immensely varied one and no easy generalisation about it is possible. It depends, first, upon the size of a church within a particular country and the character and spread of its adherents. The Catholic Church is in quite a different position *vis-à-vis* government in Zaire where its members are some 50% of the total population and where prior to independence it enjoyed a rather privileged position and Sierra Leone where it is a comparatively insignificant latecomer in a country which has anyway a numerical Moslem majority. Methodists and Presbyterians are the most established of churches in Ghana and very numerous, especially in the south; in Benin (Dahomey) nearby they are a quite small community. The pattern of colonial church-state relations varied considerably between British, French, Belgian and Portuguese possessions; and post-independence relations tend to be in part a continuation and in part a reversal of what went before. Certainly for the most part there was some form of entente between colonial governments and mission churches; it was a link between white men, frequently of the same nationality, and it has in some way continued in the white controlled south. The support of the leadership of the Dutch reformed churches is immensely valuable for the assured position of Mr Vorster and his fellow Nationalists. While the English speaking churches in South Africa have certainly been more critical of government, this has really only been true of a very small number of prominent people. Ambrose Reeves, Trevor Huddleston, Gonville ffrench-Beytagh and Colin Winter represent a distinguished line of Anglican protest in southern Africa but their position has never been characteristic of Anglican bishops, priests or laity. Indeed the fact that all four are English who could (and did) afterwards return to England is worth remembering. Archbishop Denys Hurley and Cosmas Desmond have been even more unrepresentative of Roman Catholic opinion. While there has been a series of weighty statements condemning aspects of apartheid policy, particularly from the Catholic hierarchy, it must be admitted that such statements finally carry less weight than the practical and visible acceptance of white domination within the lifestyle of the churches, whereby—for instance—it is taken as normal that churches with a very large majority of black members (say over 80% in the case of the Catholic Church) have only one or even no black diocesan bishop on a bench of ten or twenty.

The clerical and lay leadership of the main churches is effectively encapsulated within the élite, the racial minority. In South Africa the expansion of the independent churches (now accounting for some 25% of all black Christians within the Republic) can hardly be unrelated to the perception that they are clearly regarded as second class citizens within the white led churches, as they are within the state. Despite official verbal protest and the immensely sustained personal campaigns of a few individuals, the main churches do in fact provide an important spiritual sanction for the present racial division of society.

Turning to black ruled Africa, the present leadership in both state and church is too new for the hardening of quite the same pattern; nevertheless things are not as different as might be imagined. The new political and administrative leaders were largely educated in mission schools; they come from the same class and the same families as church leaders. The missions were so important an innovating force in African society that it is inevitable that the people who linked themselves most closely with them, benefiting from this new and élitist network of education and employment should constitute a sizeable part of the current establishment. There is nothing very reprehensible in that; nevertheless the consequence is that the leaders of the major churches are almost as integral a part of the governing minority in black ruled Africa as in white. The senior clergy share in the standards and status symbols of the affluent society, just as they share in many of its possibilities of power: in both ways they are only too clearly marked off from the poor and the powerless. The gift of a Mercedes from president to archbishop is now an almost ritual feature of African life.

Individual churches, while their membership may now be widely scattered across the country, very frequently have quite small areas (those in which their missions were first and most successfully established) in which most of their leadership is recruited and with which they have their strongest ties. The political influence of the church may be rather closely related to the interests of such an area. A clear example of this was in the Nigerian civil war. Biafra regarded itself as a Christian land while Nigeria as a whole has a Moslem majority even though there are many millions of Christians in other parts of the country. The Catholic Church in particular had had a strong Igbo identification and the church in the rest of the world tended to accept a little credulously a Biafran interpretation of the struggle as one for Christian survival. Igbo Catholic bishops included both hawks and doves but they all basically accepted the official Biafran political viewpoint, which is true *mutatis mutando* of 95% of bishops in any part of the world in a time of political crisis.

It is only among the smaller missions and many independent churches who recruit their members more exclusively from among the have-nots, that one may detect a rather different political outlook. Where they come into conflict with the state it is not, however, so much that they are positively encouraging anti-establishment politics, a religious ground for populism or social revolution, as that they teach too radical a withdrawal from all the interests of this world in favour of the next. The Jehovah's Witnesses, who have been banned and persecuted in several countries from Kenya to Malawi, refuse membership of the state political party or even to salute the flag. Their membership has undoubtedly a considerable appeal for poor people who feel they have next to nothing to gain from the established politics of this world and willingly turn drastically away, even at the cost of persecution, to prepare themselves for heaven. Such groups do, however, now as in the colonial past provide a possible base for populist political protest.

If the larger churches share in many ways in the affluence and attitudes to power of the ruling minority of modern Africa, they retain nevertheless a core of otherness which can be illustrated by the amount of church–state conflict which has arisen in these years. In some of it, of course, the church is present almost incidentally—precisely as part of a given segment of society. Thus seventeen Hutu priests were executed without trial in 1972 in Burundi following the Hutu rebellion, but then nearly three hundred nurses and medical assistants were also killed, and at least 100,000 people in all. While individual Christians stood out heroically in one way and another, as a whole the church in Burundi (in which over 70% of the population is Christian) was simply swept along by tribal fears in what were some of the most terrible events of modern African history.

More direct conflict may arise because an increasingly totalitarian government cannot brook a rival; in the recent past mission churches certainly at times behaved as if they formed an *imperium in imperio* and in many countries today they remain the only organisations of any size and prestige to escape effective government control. Such considerations help to explain only too well the onslaught that Mobutu in Zaire has directed at the churches, the Catholic Church especially, in 1972 and again in 1974. The churches retain their capacity for providing a point of view other than that of the one party and for mobilising people quite effectively to work in a variety of directions; they retain too a prestige related both to their high spiritual claims and the devotedness of many of their ministers which can make them seem peculiarly dangerous to governments, both of the right wing and of the left—particularly in a time of disillusion when the projects of government are being only too obviously tainted both by inefficiency and by corruption. A bishop by his mere existence may remind people of the possibility of a different future and if Archbishop Tchidimbo of Conakry has been kept in prison by the Marxist Sekou Toure since January 1971, three Anglican bishops have been expelled in succession from Namibia: Robert Mize in 1968, Colin Winter in 1972 and Richard Wood in 1975.

How do the churches envisage their own role in Africa within the wider political and economic arena? Some, doubtless, do not think about it at all, concentrating upon other areas of life and thought, but for the larger churches who do there are a number of models which present themselves, inevitably overlapping while

85

providing somewhat different stresses. There is, first of all, the model of personal inspiration. The spiritual life of the Church together with its basic doctrine inspire its members, including politicians, with high ideals, a mature sense of responsibility, a commitment to the quest for a more humane society. It could well be claimed that in many parts of Africa this task has not been badly fulfilled, even if some of the political leaders have since given up their church membership, but much of the most respected political leadership in contemporary Africa has been stimulated by one or another tradition of churchmanship. Behind the thinking of Léopold Senghor, the father of so many creative strands in modern African political thinking, lies Jacques Maritain and Teilhard de Chardin; behind that of Kaunda both his Presbyterian origins and his friendship with Colin Morris; behind Nyerere's socialism not only Senghor but a good deal of Catholic social theory. Whether it be Dr Busia or Sir Louis Mbanefo, the Igbo elder statesman, General Gowon or Bishop Muzorewa, one can detect the unmistakeable inspiration of one brand or another of missionary Christianity—sometimes more conservative, sometimes more radical, but always profoundly serious.

Beyond the inspiration of individuals, many people these last years have sought a more coherent model for the role the churches should play within society and particularly within societies so poor and so unequal as are most in Africa. With what theory and what strategy are they to show an effective concern for justice, peace, freedom? 'Members of religious organisations must encourage and help the people to co-operate together in whatever action is necessary for their development. What this will mean in practice will vary from one country to another, and from one part of a country to another part. Sometimes it will mean helping the people to form and to run their own co-operative villages. Sometimes it will mean helping the people to form their own trade unions— and not Catholic trade unions, but trade unions of workers regardless of religion. Sometimes it will mean the Church leaders involving themselves in nationalist freedom movements and being part of those movements. Sometimes it will mean co-operating with local governments or other authorities; sometimes it will mean working in opposition to established authorities and powers. Always it means the Church being on the side of social justice and helping men to live together and work together for their common good.' That is Julius Nyerere's advice to a group of Maryknoll Sisters gathered in New York in October 1970.

Development, Reconciliation, Liberation—these are the themes which come back again and again in this borderland of church and politics. Let us take them one by one. 'Development' was very much the key work for Africa in the later 1960s (as it had been for Latin America ten years earlier), and the churches in general committed themselves to it with little reservation. 'Development is the new name of Peace' said Pope Paul enthusiastically when he arrived in Uganda in July 1969. One year before, July 1968, Kenneth Kaunda had addressed the World Council of Churches in Uppsala: 'Development is a moral issue, just as it is a social and economic one. It is a challenge to the Christian conscience. Therefore the guidance and leadership of the Church during the current crisis is as strategic and invaluable as that of governments.' 'Development' justified a new preoccupation of church workers with social and economic projects just at a time when the churches were losing their traditional hold on the educational system. But it could itself take very different forms. Every kind of advance can, after all, be included under this umbrella word. Does the massive injection of foreign capital into western style industrial projects, clearly providing prestige symbols of 'modernisation' but rather few local jobs, constitute a worth while form of development? The development debate quickly becomes one concerning intermediate technology, the distribution of income, class structure and whether a poor society is helped or harmed by an increase in its national income if the increase touches only the tiny few. 'Development' in fact can only too easily enlarge the inequality between rich and poor and in the third world (Latin America especially) the word has almost come to have a bad smell about it—as suggesting no more than the kind side of capitalist strategy: improvement must not be allowed to assail the structures of inequality.

Such a criticism is partly fair, partly unfair. Church workers all over Africa have certainly thrown themselves into development projects, generally of a small scale type, with zeal and considerable success: co-operatives, credit unions, village polytechnics, small farming schemes. In this they have been aided by international or western bodies such as OXFAM, Christian Aid, MISEREOR and CARITAS. Naturally such projects will be sited particularly in the poorest and most underprivileged areas of society—depressed rural areas or urban shanty towns such as Nairobi's Mathare Valley. They can hardly succeed without a wider action of socio-political education—the conscientisation of Paulo Freire in fact. The further they go, the more success they have, the greater the challenge they are bound to mount towards existing oppressive structures in society, the vast imbalance of wealth. Again, if the Church sponsors (and, maybe, provides a book-keeper for) a successful honey-producing co-operative in a sparsely populated forest area, it can quickly become yet again a powerful secular force in the district and appear as a threat to local Party officials. Only too easily may the co-operative be taken over by the latter and allowed to fall to pieces through lack of interest or inefficiency. However much projects of development start with an acceptance of the structures of society as they are in a fairly apolitical way, if they are really effective they can steadily draw those committed to them into the more revolutionary paths of liberation.

The conflict of human interests, whether tribal, racial or class, is central to the whole issue. The first Christian response to conflict is to take up the task of reconciliation. This can seem most obvious in situations of civil war, but here as everywhere the problems inherent in an effective dynamic of mediation are im-mense. Church leaders may already have committed themselves too deeply to one side to be acceptable go-betweens to the other. It is almost impossible both to provide humanitarian aid to the weaker side and be accepted as a mediator by the stronger. The churches tend to take up the former role more quickly, as being urgent and uncomplicated, and then find that it baulks the latter. This was certainly the case in regard to Nigeria where the Federal authorities felt strongly that church agencies by their activities and some church leaders by their remarks had committed themselves irretrievably to the Biafran cause. In the case of the Sudanese civil war, on the other hand, ecclesiastical mediation, carried out by Canon Burgess Carr and the All Africa Conference of Churches, was more effective in contributing to an end to the conflict through the Addis Ababa talks of 1972. Here, however, the war had gone on far longer, reaching an effective stalemate, so that both sides were more ready to compromise; moreover the churches had been publicly identified less with the Anyanya than they were with Biafra. If the AACC can be praised for its contribution to final reconciliation, it and other church agencies might equally be blamed for doing too little to help the southern Sudanese over many earlier years.

Humanly speaking reconciliation hardly seems possible before there is a certain balance of power or, alternatively, until the political struggle has been essentially resolved one way or the other. Thus in the Nigerian case a most remarkable reconciliation has been achieved at the human level, but only after the end of the war and the collapse of Biafra. While the institutional churches did not contribute much to this, individuals surely did, and the Christian spirit of General Gowon himself must be reckoned a major factor in the absence of vindictiveness shown by the victorious Federalists.

Helping a weaker, oppressed side is not compatible with holding a balance of impartiality as reconciler; if one side is in such a position, the immediate Christian task may be to give it all possible help—to liberate, in fact, rather than to reconcile: to get the oppressor off the back of the oppressed. Only when a certain balance is achieved may the wider task of reconciliation be a feasible one. On this line of thinking, 'reconciliation' like 'development' leads through to 'liberation' and explains the conviction of some Christians that there is no other course open than to commit themselves to a struggle—particularly in the racial context of southern Africa—which involves a major overturning of the present political and economic structures.

Speaking to the Maryknoll Sisters in 1970 President Nyerere declared 'My purpose today is to suggest to you that the Church should accept that the development of peoples means rebellion . . . unless we participate actively in the rebellion against those social structures and economic organisation which condemn men to poverty, humiliation and degradation, then the Church will become irrelevant to man.' The same year the World Council of Churches made its first grants for humanitarian purposes to Frelimo and other liberation movements. This was a European and American rather than an African decision, but it has polarised Christian opinion both in Africa and elsewhere as few other decisions have ever done. Hitherto there had been a fairly steadily suggested identification of the cause of white supremacy in southern Africa with that of 'Christian civilisation' and even in 1975 Mr Vorster could insist that South African involvement in Angola was to free men of 'the yoke of atheist communist enslavement'. Yet here was the World Council, a body with undeniably great authority, actually suggesting by its grants that the Christian interest was to be found upon the other side. While white led churches in South Africa protested vehemently against the grants, the Protestant churches of the continent in general overwhelmingly supported them at the Lusaka Assembly of May 1974.

Yet in Africa as a whole there has hitherto been no general upsurge of Christian liberationists, such as has happened in Latin America. The nearest equivalent to what has taken place in South America may be found among the little group of Catholic priests in Mozambique who during the last, most oppressive, years of Portuguese rule there provided a striking and powerful witness, both protesting against military atrocities and calling for a total change of regime. It was for doing these things that the Spanish Fathers, Alfonso Valverde and Martin Hernandez, spent 1972 and 1973 untried in Machava concentration camp. In May 1972 a Portuguese priest, Fr Luis Afonso da Costa, penned the following desperate words from his mission at Boroma near Tete in support of his Spanish colleagues. He was at once expelled the country. 'We missionaries are for peace and against war. We refuse to accept the state of war in which the country is being held. Therefore they persecute us. We are not allowed to write in order to enlighten public opinion as to this anachronistic situation of permanent injustice. Nevertheless we claim this right and we speak in the name of those who have no voice—the oppressed, the tortured, the massacred.'

It is in Rhodesia that senior church leaders have come nearest to full identification with the cause of political liberation. While the bishops of the Catholic Church, and most notably Donal Lamont of Umtali, have been regularly and sternly critical of the Smith government—so that white Catholics have even written to Rome seeking Bishop Lamont's removal—it is Bishop Abel Muzorewa of the Methodist Episcopal Church whose role has been most forthright. The successor to an American bishop deported by Ian Smith, Muzorewa was quite clearly an ecclesiastical figure without prior political experience. He was the senior African ecclesiastic in the country at a time of national crisis—the Home–Smith settlement proposals, late 1971. With all the leading African politicians either in detention or in exile, Muzorewa was called to chair the newly established African National Council whose membership cut right across traditional political divisions. His wise, quiet but forceful leadership for over three years held his people together in the basic aim of liberation while being steadily open to negotiation. Nevertheless as divisions old and new re-established themselves within the ANC Muzorewa found it increasingly difficult to maintain his nonpartisan role and in the course of 1975 succumbed to identification with the Sithole faction, thus extinguishing his true political *raison d'être*. His story is a fascinating but tragic object lesson in the problems inherent in church leadership within the arena of political liberation.

In the Republic of South Africa the possibility of armed revolution has hitherto hardly presented itself, and its consequences would be so appalling that it is little wonder if those Christian leaders most aware of the present injustice of the situation still desperately seek some quite other way. There has never been a time when there have not been Christian voices in South Africa to protest against the severe racial discrimination in law, land ownership, political rights, educational facilities and economic opportunities, but recent years have seen a new depth and clarity in such pronouncements from several sides. The growth of 'black theology', of an African theology of liberation growing out of the experience of poverty, rejection and suffering, may be its present most important expression. Most theologians in Africa as in Europe and America are professionally in the 'Dives' category, men with considerable salaries and social status. The writers of black theology are, on the contrary, expelled seminarians, pastors banned from their pulpits, students sent down from their universities. They are, one may say, out with Lazarus. They write from the world of the poor, not from that of the rich. 'Black theology' can both challenge 'African theology' and be criticised by it. The African theologian in Nigeria or Kenya stressing the religious and cultural continuity with Africa's past which provides the key theme for his writing, will criticise 'black theology' as being of limited relevance in comparison: it is only for a time and a place. When South Africa is liberated it will have no more point. But the black theologian replies that liberation does not only need to take place in South Africa; the poor are everywhere and 'black theology' may be quite as relevant to the vast inequalities of Nigeria as to those of the south. Oppression did not start with the white man and Africa today may need to seek liberation not only in but from the weight of its own tradition. Black theology, by starting with oppression and poverty, is bound to be centrally concerned with sin and redemption and so with Christ and the interpretation of suffering in the cross—all themes which appear rather marginal in the 'African theology' of West and East Africa. In this context the latter, instead of appearing as intended as a radical challenge to the colonial-missionary establishment, may seem instead to be dangerously encapsulated by the current preoccupations of the new élite, an unrealistic idealisation of the past;

it can suggest preoccupation with affronts from long dead missionaries, rather than with those crying human problems of the post-independence era—which reveal with such poignancy the enduring tragedy of the human condition.

In July 1974 the South African Council of Churches passed a resolution at Hammanskraal calling on the churches to invite their white members to consider the moral duty of conscientious objection. Thus, for the first time, a gospel of non-violence was proposed in clear terms in southern Africa to white as well as black. It did, of course, produce a very sharp reaction from government about to be faced with a Frelimo takeover in Mozambique next door. The resolution was proposed by Dr Beyers Naudé, director of the Christian Institute, who had been himself on trial in a Pretoria court eight months earlier. More than any other man he has taken the lead these last years in challenging the apartheid state in the name of Christ. Member of an old and respected Afrikaner family, former minister and moderator in the *Nederduits Gereformeerde Kerk*, his challenge has come from the very heart of the system and has had about it a consistency, a quality of personal anguish, and a depth of Christian conviction invariably expressed with the greatest care and moderation, which have given it profound weight both in secular and ecclesiastical circles. When he refused to testify before a parliamentary commission held in secret to investigate the activities of the Christian Institute, he was brought to trial in November 1973 for preferring divine to civil obedience: 'When the Government deviates from the Gospel, the Christian is bound by his conscience to resist it.'

While in varying circumstances churchmen in Africa have applied to their work the models of development, reconciliation and liberation, it may be that the most significant model is rather one of challenge—though challenge, too, will of course take various forms. While Christians rightly feel called to participate in many movements, some directed by governments, some directed against governments, there is clearly an abiding danger that the church becomes so tied up with a particular government in its development plans, a particular liberation movement in its struggle to end oppression, that it loses its capacity of independent criticism, of being specifically itself. The church's greatest need may be to avoid such an identification with any individual political movement that it loses its own freedom of witness—and this can apply even in regard to the most high minded of governments. There is a deep tendency towards the monolithic and the totalitarian in Africa today and the most valuable contribution of the church to society may be seen as the provision of an alternative: an alternative voice, source of information, criterion for judgement, for the ordering of priorities and ultimate loyalties. To some extent this requires the provision of room for employment, a certain breathing space for hard pressed individuals not controllable by a government department. Such an alternative can be very challenging and the powers that be may do their best to suppress it.

If this be so, then the churches may provide no more valuable service in Africa today than the contribution of an independent press—almost every other newspaper is firmly under government control in most black ruled countries. *Afrique Nouvelle* published in Dakar in the security of Senghor's rather liberal regime but circulating all across French speaking West Africa is perhaps the most important of all. But *Target* in Kenya, *Kiongozi* in Tanzania, *Munno* in Uganda and a number of other church papers are all performing an immensely important task in offering, often with a great deal of discretion, an independent vision from within local society. It is not surprising that Mobutu closed all church connected newspapers in his campaign to stifle the independent influence of the churches in Zaire. The task of the editor of a Christian paper who sees it in this way is an extremely dangerous and exposed one. Seeiso Serutla, editor of the Protestant *Leselinyana* in Lesotho, was arrested and his paper banned when it took up a critical line against the government of Chief Jonathan in the election of 1970. Father Clement Kiggundu, editor of the Luganda *Munno*, was found murdered in his car near Kampala in January 1973.

The alternative which it may finally be the church's most valuable contribution to offer society is not the alternative of another world—though the church is always subject to the temptation to reduce it to this and frequently succumbs. A straight appeal to withdrawal from this-worldly concerns is indeed a widespread phenomenon in African Christianity as elsewhere. If it limits Christian leaders to preaching about 'religious' matters, it may indeed be just what the most hardened secular ruler may desire; but if it goes further to draw Christians away from civil or political duties, it can on the contrary precipitate conflict between church and state as in the case of the Jehovah's Witnesses or, again, in that of the Zambian Lumpa Church: 'Do not look for the things of this world' was Alice Lenshina's most insistent teaching and it was only too well suited for precipitating a conflict with a raw young nationalist party anxious to harness the churches to policies entirely concerned with the development of this world's goods.

Such is not the type of alternative which most churches in Africa endeavour in an admittedly fumbling manner to provide today. They fully accept the this-worldly duties of their members, they honour their presidents and co-operate with their policies—they may indeed seem rather too willing to fall in with the vision of each: to acclaim Kenyatta in Kenya, Banda in Malawi, Mobutu in Zaire, Houphouet in Ivory Coast, Nyerere in Tanzania. But they are conscious too of standing a little apart; at least potentially able to point out the oppressiveness of a Marxist reordering of traditional village life as well as the oppressiveness of white colonialists and racialists, and the oppressiveness of some traditional structures of society too. The cult of authenticity may prove exceedingly burdensome, just as the imposition of 'scientific socialism' may turn out to be devastatingly alienating, and the church must finally find the courage to say so.

In practice the churches come to share rather too easily in one or more of such oppressions, and are often more than slow to raise their voice in protest unless there appears the major horror of a Sharpeville or a Wiriyamu. The burden of responsibility for maintaining in existence that little piercing voice of freedom and of truthful critique has generally to be borne by a much smaller and less protected group—the editor of *Target*, the Burgos Fathers in Mozambique and the Maryknoll Sisters in East Africa, Wole Soyinka, the Christian Institute. With the last named it could be that South Africa is offering a helpful model to the rest of Africa, in the Institute's self-defined role, in its relationship with the churches, in its type of leadership. Before challenging the state Beyers Naudé was compelled to challenge his own church which over the years has made every effort to silence him. His last sermon as a minister was preached in September 1963 on the text 'We must obey God rather than men'. The area of obedience in question was that of social and political justice but the men he was then referring to were not political leaders but the ecclesiastics who wished to prevent him from taking on the editorship of *Pro Veritate* and the work of the Christian Institute: 'The choice before me is not firstly a choice between pastoral work and other Christian work, not between the Church and *Pro Veritate* or the Church and the Christian Institute. No, the choice goes much deeper. It is a choice between religious conviction and submission to ecclesiastical authority. By obeying the latter unconditionally I would save face but lose my soul.' He read through the same sermon word for word ten years later when on trial in a magistrate's court in Pretoria. The men he could not obey were now the political leaders of his country and as he quietly read out his exegesis of the words of the New Testament with its immense implications, he stood perhaps for a little army of fellow Christians, black and white, up and down the continent who have—most of them—no power effectively to change the many and varied structures of poverty, injustice, inequality and oppression with which they are confronted but who are no longer able to keep silent in face of them, cost what it may. 'We must obey God rather than men.'

References and further reading

Books referred to under one chapter may, of course, be of use elsewhere, thus Daneel's two massive volumes *Old and New in Southern Shona Independent Churches* is a major reference book for all the first four chapters.

Chapter 1

A good entry into modern African Christian history lies in two essays: the first by Richard Gray, is entitled *Problems of Historical Perspectives: the Planting of Christianity in Africa in the nineteenth and twentieth centuries* and is to be found in the symposium *Christianity in Tropical Africa*, edited by C. G. Baeta (Oxford, 1968); the second, by J. F. Ajayi and E. A. Ayendele, *Writing African Church History* is one of the essays presented to Bengt Sundkler in *The Church Crossing Frontiers* (Gleerup, Uppsala, 1969). Both volumes have much else of interest for our theme; to them may be added a third symposium *African Initiatives in Religion*, edited by David Barrett (East African Publishing House, 1971).

An important basic work remains the final volumes of C. P. Groves, *The Planting of Christianity in Africa* (London, 4 vols, 1948–58), to which should be added Roland Oliver's masterly *The Missionary Factor in East Africa* (Longman, 1952). J. F. Ajayi, *Christian Missions in Nigeria 1841–1891* (Northwestern University Press, 1965), E. A. Ayendele, *The Missionary Impact on Modern Nigeria 1842–1914* (Longman, 1966), and F. K. Ekechi, *Missionary Enterprise and Rivalry in Igboland 1857–1914* (Frank Cass, 1972), are three major Nigerian contributions to missionary historiography. John V. Taylor, *The Growth of the Church in Buganda* (SCM, 1958), R. Slade, *English-Speaking Missions in the Congo Independent State 1878–1908* (Brussels, 1959), Marcia Wright, *German Missions in Tanganyika 1891–1941*

97

(Oxford, 1971), F. L. Bartels, *The Roots of Ghana Methodism* (Cambridge, 1965), J. Taylor and D. Lehmann, *Christians of the Copperbelt* (SCM, 1961), and Ian Linden, *Catholics, Peasants and Chewa Resistance in Nyasaland* (Heinemann, 1974), are a selection from among the many recent studies on church growth in particular countries.

The seven hundred pages of *Outlook on a Century, South Africa 1879–1970*, edited by Francis Wilson and Dominique Perrot (Lovedale Press, 1973) is a splendid source book for church and society in the south. T. A. Beetham, *Christianity and the New Africa* (Pall Mall, 1967), provides an overall view of the way things looked in the mid-1960s.

Bengt Sundkler, *Bantu Prophets in South Africa* (Oxford, first edition 1948, second edition 1961), was a seminal work in a field where there is now a vast literature. On the more historical side the following may be singled out: J. B. Webster, *The African Churches among the Yoruba 1888–1922* (Oxford, 1964), G. Shepperson and T. Price, *Independent African* (Edinburgh, 1958), F. Welbourne and B. Ogot, *A Place to Feel at Home* (Oxford, 1966), G. Haliburton, *The Prophet Harris* (Longman, 1971), and Marie-Louise Martin, *Kimbangu* (Blackwell, 1975).

For a recent critical study of Simon Kimbangu, about whom there are now hundreds of published studies, see Cecilia Irvine, 'The Birth of the Kimbanguist Movement in the Bas-Zaire 1921', *Journal of Religion in Africa*, 1974, pp. 23–76.

Finally, *Themes in the Christian History of Central Africa*, edited by T. Ranger and J. Weller (Heinemann, 1975), shows as well as any single volume can the current concerns of the African church historian.

Chapter 2

Much of the information in and behind this chapter comes from a range of ecclesiastical directories, news-sheets and such-like. The pages of AFER (African Ecclesiastical Review) published regularly since 1959 (present address: Amecea Pastoral Institute, P.O. Box 908, Eldoret, Kenya) is a mine of valuable information and comment, especially for the Roman Catholic side. The *Kenya Churches Handbook*, published in 1973 by the Research Department of the National Christian Council of Kenya is unique of its kind. P. Bolink, *Towards Church Union in Zambia* (Holland, 1967), is a detailed study of ecumenical progress in one country; A. Hastings, *Church and Mission in Modern Africa* (Burns Oates and Fordham, 1967), and some chapters of the author's *Mission and Ministry* (Sheed & Ward, 1971), treat principally of the Catholic Church, as does Bishop P. Kalilombe's booklet *Christ's Church in Lilongwe Today and Tomorrow* (Amecea, 1973), which is quoted in the text.

The two volumes already published of M. L. Daneel, *Old and New in Southern Shona Independent Churches* (Mouton, 1971 and 1974), H. Turner's two volumed *African Independent Church* (Oxford, 1967) B. Sundkler, *Zulu Zion* (Oxford, 1976), and J. Peel, *Aladura: A Religious Movement among the Yoruba* (Oxford, 1968) provide the most impressive recent studies of the organisation and thought of some independent churches. David Beckmann, *Eden Revival* (Concordia, 1975) is a shorter account of one Ghanaian spiritual church. G. Oosthuizen, *The Theology of a South African Messiah* (Leiden, 1967), is the source for the hymn of Isaiah Shembe quoted in the chapter. A useful discussion of the relative absence of independency in Tanzania is to be found in two works of T. Ranger, *The African Churches of Tanzania* (Historical Association of Tanzania, 1969), and *Christian Independency in Tanzania*, pp. 122–45 of D. Barrett, *African Initiatives in Religion* (Nairobi, 1971).

Chapter 3

Two recent books by Fr Aylward Shorter form a good introduction here: *African Culture and the Christian Church* (Geoffrey Chapman, 1973) and *African Christian Theology* (Geoffrey Chapman, 1975). Among the writings of contemporary African theologians the following may be singled out: John Mbiti, *African Religions and Philosophy* (Heinemann, 1969), and *Concepts of God in Africa* (SPCK, 1970), E. Bolaji Idowu, *African Traditional Religion* (SCM, 1973), Harry Sawyerr, *Creative Evangelism* (Lutterworth, 1968), and *God, Ancestor or Creator?* (Longmans, 1970). The essays in honour of Harry Sawyerr entitled *New Testament Christianity for Africa and for the World*, edited by M. Glasswell and E. Fashole-Luke (SPCK, 1974) include a number of useful pieces.

On Christianity and society one may refer to Monica Wilson's *Religion and the Transformation of Society* (Cambridge, 1971),

W. Sangree, *Age, Prayer and Politics in Tiriki, Kenya* (Oxford, 1966), A. Hastings, *Christian Marriage in Africa* (SPCK, 1973), E. Hillman, *Polygamy Reconsidered* (Orbis, 1975), Marshall Murphree, *Christianity and the Shona* (1969), and a collection of essays published in honour of Monica Wilson and entitled *Religion and Social Change in southern Africa* (Rex Collings, 1975), edited by M. Whisson and M. West.

Two classical studies of traditional African religion remain E. Evans-Pritchard, *Nuer Religion* (Oxford, 1956), and G. Lienhardt, *Divinity and Experience, the Religion of the Dinka* (Oxford, 1961). A major recent symposium is *The Historical Study of African Religion*, edited by T. Ranger and I. Kimambo (Heinemann, 1972).

Chapter 4

One starting point here is Robin Horton's article 'African Traditional Thought and Western Science' in *Africa*, 1967, pp. 50–71 and 155–87. Amid a very considerable literature one may refer to Lucy Mair, *Witchcraft* (World University Library, 1969), *Witchcraft and Sorcery in East Africa*, edited by J. Middleton and E. Winter (Routledge & Kegan Paul, 1963), *Witchcraft Confessions and Accusations*, edited by Mary Douglas (Tavistock, 1970), Norman Cohn, *Europe's Inner Demons, an Enquiry inspired by the great witch-hunt* (Chatto-Heinemann, 1975), J. Crawford, *Witchcraft and Sorcery in Rhodesia* (Oxford, 1967), and *Spirit Mediumship and Society in Africa*, edited by J. Beattie and J. Middleton (Routledge & Kegan Paul, 1969).

M. L. Daneel, *Zionism and Faith-Healing in Rhodesia* (Mouton, 1970), describes Bishop Mutendi's headquarters; this can be compared with J. Fernandez, 'The Precincts of the Prophet. A Day with Johannes Galilee Shembe', *Journal of Religion in Africa*, 1973, pp. 32–53; T. Ranger's account of Mwana Lesa is to be found on pp. 45–75 of *Themes in the Christian History of Central Africa*, edited by T. Ranger and J. Weller. The best account of Alice Lenshina is by Andrew Roberts, *The Lumpa Church of Alice Lenshina* (Lusaka, 1972). Dr Erivwo has written on 'Christian Attitudes to Witchcraft' in AFER, 1975, pp. 23–30, and Fr Singleton, 'Confession of an Extempore Exorcist', AFER, 1975, pp. 303–9.

The lynching in Herbert Macaulay Street was reported in

the Lagos *Evening Times*, 12 September 1975; the remarks of Kamwi, the Mambova headman, come from the *Times of Zambia*, 28 August 1971; the Rhodesian case of the prophet Kiwanyana is to be found in Crawford, p. 229.

Chapter 5

The very large literature on modern African politics and economics refers on occasion to the position of the churches, but there is little systematic treatment which has been published. One may refer to Nyerere's various volumes of essays, especially *Man and Development* (Oxford, 1974), which includes his important address to the Maryknoll Sisters, and Kaunda's *Letter to my Children* (Longman, 1973), which was quoted in the text. Jacques Hymans' 'intellectual biography' of *Léopold Sédar Senghor* (Edinburgh, 1971), may be noted. Ndabaningi Sithole's biography of *Obed Mutezo, the Mudzimi Christian Nationalist* (Oxford, 1970) is a truly remarkable work.

A. Hastings, *Wiriyamu* (Search, 1974), documents the church's political position in Mozambique during the final years of Portuguese rule; to it may be added the author's 'Christianity and Revolution', *African Affairs*, 1975, pp. 347–61, and 'A Typology of church–state relations', pp. 47–67 of *The Faces of God* (Geoffrey Chapman, 1975). Two famous South African trials of churchmen are treated in Gonville ffrench-Beytagh, *Encountering Darkness* (Collins, 1973), and *The Trial of Beyers Naudé* (Search Press, 1975). *Black Theology, the South African voice*, has been edited by Basil Moore (Hurst, 1973), to which should be added David Bosch, 'Currents and Crosscurrents in South African Black Theology', *Journal of Religion in Africa*, 1974, pp. 1–22. Recent developments in Uganda are treated by Akiiki B. Mujaju, 'The Political Crisis of Church Institutions in Uganda', *African Affairs*, 1976, pp. 67–85.

Index

Abidjan, 17, 79
Acheampong, Colonel, 79
Achebe, Chinua, 57
Achimota, 8
Addis Ababa, 88
African Apostolic Church, 54
Aggrey, James, 8
Agossou, Medewale-Jacob, 58
Aiyetoro, 1
Akinsowon, Abiodun, 12
Aladura, 1, 12, 27–8, 53, 72
All Africa Conference of Churches, 17–18, 22–3, 88–9
Amin, Idi, 15, 18, 81
Anglicans, 1–3, 12, 18–19, 21, 28–9, 60, 83
Angola, 29, 32, 79, 89
Apostolic Revelation Society, 26
Aupiais, Fr, 42

Bagamoyo, 4
Bamalaki, 70
Banda, Kamuzu, 79, 94
Baptists, 1, 11, 29
Bobo-Dioulasso, 58
Boroma, 90
Botswana, 3
Buganda, 4, 7
Bukoba, 33
Burgos Fathers, 90, 94
Burundi, 14–15, 24, 32, 77, 85
Busia, Dr, 80, 86

Calabar, 24, 66
Cameroon, 24, 49
Canterbury Cathedral, 2, 19
Carr, Burgess, 23, 88
Catholics, 1–3, 5, 7, 11, 17, 19, 21, 25, 28, 31–5, 82–5, 90
Celestial Church of Christ, 54
Chad, 79
Cherubim and Seraphim, 12, 72
Christ Apostolic Church, 72

Christian Institute, 92, 94
Church Missionary Society (CMS) 2, 4
Church of the Lord (Aladura), 27–8, 72
Conakry, 85
Congo, 11, 29
Congregationalists, 3, 18
Crowther, Samuel Ajayi, 2–4, 7

Da Costa, Luis Afonso, 90
Dahomey (now Benin), 32, 42, 58, 81, 82
Dakar, 93
Dery, Peter, 48, 59
Desmond, Cosmas, 83
Dialungana, Solomon, 27
Diangienda, Joseph, 12, 27, 71
Dutch Reformed, 3, 83, 92

Eden Revival, 1
Egypt, 1–2
Ekuphakameni, 26–7
Engulu, citizen, 58
Enugu, 34
Erivwo, S., 73
Ethiopia, 1–2, 17, 40, 79
Eyadema, General, 80–1

Fasholé-Luke, Edward, 58
ffrench-Beytagh, Gonville, 83
Fiwila, 60
Fort Hare, 7–8
Fourah Bay, 2
Freeman, Thomas Birch, 2
Freetown, 2
Frelimo, 15, 57, 81-2, 92

Gabon, 1
Gatu, John, 22
Ghana, 2, 8, 24, 26, 28–9, 32, 48, 56, 71, 79–80, 82
Gold Coast (see Ghana) 2, 8, 10, 12
Gowon, General, 86, 89

Grahamstown, 3

Hammanskraal, 92
Harris, William Wadé, 10–12
Hernandez, Martin, 90
Hinderer, David, 3
Holy Ghost Fathers, 4
Houphouet-Boigny, President, 79, 94
Huddleston, Trevor, 83
Hurley, Denys, 83

Ibadan, 17
Idowu, Bolaji, 50, 58, 73–4
Ivory Coast, 10, 94

Jabavu, D. D. T., 8
Jabavu, J. Tengo, 7–8
Jehovah's Witnesses, 84, 93
Jehu-Appiah, Jemisimiham, 12
John, Edmund, 62–3
Johnson, James, 40

Kalilombe, Patrick, 34, 58
Kampala, 17, 59, 93
Kaunda, David, 7, 77
Kaunda, Kenneth, 7, 14, 61, 77, 79, 86–7
Kayibanda, Grégoire, 77
Kayoya, Michel, 14–15
Kenya, 22, 24–5, 28, 33, 50, 55, 57, 71, 78, 84, 91, 93–4
Kenyatta, Jomo, 14, 79, 94
Kerekou, T., 81
Khambule, George, 27
Kiggundu, Clement, 93
Kimbangu, Simon, 1, 11–12, 26, 71
Kimbanguists, 1, 12, 17–19, 27, 32, 53
Kinshasa, 27, 32
Kisangani, 32
Kivebulaya, Apolo, 7
Kiwanuka, Benedicto, 15
Kuruman, 3

Lagos, 12, 55, 60
Lake Eni, 68
Lambarene, 1
Lamont, Donal, 90
Lavigerie, Cardinal, 4
Laws, Robert, 4

Lekhanyane, Enginasi, 71
Lenshina, Alice, 1, 61–3, 93
Lesotho, 3, 32, 93
Liberia, 10, 23, 48
Lilongwe, 34, 58
Livingstone, David, 3–4
Livingstonia, 4, 7–8, 60
London Missionary Society, 3
Lovedale, 8
Lubwa, 7, 77
Lumpa Church, 61–2, 93
Lusaka, 17, 22–3, 77, 89
Lutherans, 1, 21, 30, 48

Machava, 15, 90
Machel, Samora, 80–2
Mackenzie, Bishop, 4
Magila, 4
Malawi, 24, 34, 57–8, 84, 94
Malula, Cardinal, 14, 37
Mambova, 63
Manganhela, Zedequias, 15
Maranke, Johane, 54, 59
Maria Legio, 1, 25, 28
Maritain, Jacques, 86
Maryknoll Sisters, 86, 89, 94
Masaka, 7
Mbanefo, Sir Louis, 86
Mboga, 7
Mbunga, Stephen, 48
Methodists, 1–3, 11, 18, 21, 25, 28–9, 31, 42, 82, 90
Micombero, Michel, 77
Mize, Robert, 85
Mobutu, Sese Seko, 14, 18, 32, 37, 43, 53, 58–9, 79, 85, 93–4
Moffat, Robert, 3
Mombasa, 4
Morris, Colin, 86
Moshi, 33
Mozambique, 15, 32, 57, 79, 81, 90, 92, 94
Musaka, Victor, 7
Mulago, Vincent gwa Cikala Musharhamina, 37
Multimedia Zambia, 18–19
Musama Disco Christo Church, 12, 28
Mutendi, Samuel, 26, 70–1
Mutesa, King, 4

Muzorewa, Abel, 14, 86, 90

Nairobi, 1, 23, 79, 87
Namibia, 85
Namugongo, 17
Natal, 26
Naudé, Beyers, 2, 92, 94
Ndzon-Melen, 49
Neto, Agostinho, 80
Ngugi, James, 57
Niger, 2
Nigeria, 1–2, 5, 12–14, 18, 24–5, 28–9, 31–2, 34, 37, 40, 45, 50, 53, 57, 68, 71, 79, 84, 88–9, 91
N'Kamba, 11, 26
Nkomo, Joshua, 14
Nyabadza, Basil, 75
Nyabadza, Francis, 75
Nyamiti, Charles, 58
Nyerere, Julius, 1, 14, 43, 58, 77–8, 82, 86, 89, 94
Nyirenda, Tomo, 60–1, 63

Obote, Milton, 15, 77
Okot p'Bitek, 51
Onitsha, 34
Opoku-pare, Emanuel, 56
Orimolade, Moses, 12
Oshitelu, Josiah, 12, 71–2
Owerri, 34

Paul VI, 17, 59, 77, 87
Presbyterians, 1–2, 15, 18, 21–2, 29, 60, 82, 86

Reeves, Ambrose, 83
Rhodesia, 3, 24, 26, 41–2, 54, 70, 73, 75, 79–80, 90
Rwanda, 14, 24, 32, 77

Sacred Order of the Silent Brotherhood, 56
Sanon, Anselm, 58
Sastre, Robert, 58
Sawyerr, Harry, 50
Schweitzer, Albert, 1
Senegal 2–3, 17
Senghor, Léopold, 1, 41, 57, 79, 86, 93
Serutla, Seeiso, 93
Sharpeville, 94
Shembe, Isaiah, 26–7, 71

Shembe, Johannes Galilee, 71
Shorter, Aylward, 49
Sierra Leone, 3, 24, 50, 82
Sithole, Ndabaningi, 14, 90
Smith, Edwin, 42
Smith, Ian, 79, 90
Soga, Tiyo, 3, 8
Songea, 33
South Africa, 12, 17, 24–5, 59, 71, 78–80, 83, 89, 91, 94
Soyinka, Wole, 57, 94
Streicher, Bishop, 7
Sudan, 14, 17, 79, 88
Sumbawanga, 33

Tadzewu, 26
Tanzania, 24, 30, 32–3, 57, 62–3, 77, 79–80, 82, 93–4
Tchidimbo, Archbishop, 85
Teilhard de Chardin, Pierre, 86
Tete, 90
Tiriki, 55
Togo, 32, 80–1
Touré, Sekou, 81, 85
Tshibangu, T., 50, 58

Uganda, 15, 24, 29, 32, 57, 70, 77, 87, 93
Umuahia, 34
United Church of Zambia, 18
Universities Mission to Central Africa, 4
Upper Volta, 32, 58, 78

Valverde, Alfonso, 90
Vorster, John, 79, 83, 89

White Fathers, 4
Winter, Colin, 83, 85
Wiriyamu, 94
Wood, Richard, 85
World Council of Churches, 1, 87, 89
Wovenu, Charles Kobla, 26

Zaire, 1, 12–13, 18, 24, 26, 29, 32, 37, 49–50, 58–9, 71, 79–80, 82, 85, 93–4
Zambia, 1, 4, 7, 18, 57, 60–1, 63, 77, 80, 93
Zanzibar, 4
Zimbabwe, 42